Craft Your Path To Success

The Business of Making Money

Making Arts and Crafts

PAUL RILEY

UKCraftFairs Ltd

Copyright © 2017 Paul Riley

The moral right of the author has been asserted

All rights reserved. Apart from any use permitted under UK copyright law, this publication may only be reproduced, stored, or transmitted, in any form, or by any means, with prior permission in writing of the publishers or, in the case of reprographic production, in accordance with the terms of licences issued by the Copyright Licensing Agency.

ISBN: 978-0-9957058-1-4

Published by UKCraftFairs Ltd

UKCraftFairs Ltd, Airport House, Purley Way, Croydon CR0 0XZ

publishing@ukcraftfairs.com

Visit our website at www.UKCraftFairs.com

This book is for information purposes only and does not constitute legal, financial, tax, accountancy, technical, business or any other form of professional advice. The information is presented without any warranty or guarantee regarding completeness or accuracy and the author and publisher assume no responsibility for errors or omissions. The author and publisher accept no responsibility for any liability, risk, loss, damages, or other consequences, personal or otherwise, which arise, either directly or indirectly, from the information in this book. You should seek legal, financial, tax, accountancy, technical, business and all other advice from competent appropriately qualified professionals, who understand your situation.

To family and the business we build together

Contents

INTRODUCTION	11
CHAPTER 1 GETTING STARTED	13
Foundations of Success	13
Starting Small	15
Products and Services	16
Becoming Self Employed	17
Sole Trader and Sole Proprietorship	18
Business Partnership	18
Limited Company and Limited Liability Company	19
Limited Company in the United Kingdom	19
Limited Liability Company in the United States	20
Business Plan	21
Market Research	22
Mission Statement and Vision Statement	23
Business Name	25
Branding	26
Work Space	26
Business Insurance	28
Health and Safety	29
Data Security	30
Personal Skills and Resources	31
Employing Other People	33
Team Building	34
Business Organisations and Networks	34
CHAPTER 2 MANAGING YOUR FINANCES	37
Business Finances	37
Business Bank Account	38
Startup Finance	39
Startup Costs	40
Fixed Costs	41

    Variable Costs   41
    Managing Cash Flow   41
    Taxes in the United Kingdom   43
    Taxes in the United States   45

CHAPTER 3 LIFE AND WORK   49
    Your Ideal Job or Business   49
    Education and Work   51
    Social Intelligence   53
    Emotional Intelligence   55
    Physical Intelligence   55
    Ethical Intelligence   56
    Work Life Balance   56
    Self-belief   57
    Fulfilling Work   58
    Happiness   60

CHAPTER 4 PATHS TO SUCCESS   61
    Finding Your Path   61
    Formative Years   61
    Finding Your Way   62
    Learning Skills   63
    Human Society   66
    The Creative Process   68
    Achieving Your Potential   70
    Personal Development   71
    The Art of Doing Nothing   73
    Time and Money   73
    Resistance To Change   75
    Decision Making   76
    Celebrate Success   76

CHAPTER 5 YOUR CUSTOMERS   79
    Attracting Customers   79
    Your Audience   79
    Customer Surveys   80
    Customer Communications   81

Premium Products and Services	82
Email Marketing	84
Customer Data	86
Managing Complaints	88
Recommendations Reviews and Testimonials	89
CHAPTER 6 YOUR BUSINESS WEBSITE	**91**
Do You Need A Website?	91
Website Technology	91
Domain Names	92
Planning Your Website	93
From Planning to Deployment	95
Website Visitor Engagement	96
Web Design	97
Creating Your Website	98
Content Management Systems	98
Open Source CMS or Proprietary CMS	99
Drupal and Wordpress	101
Hosting Your Website	102
CHAPTER 7 PRICING YOUR WORK	**106**
Pricing Decisions	106
Cost Price	106
Sales Costs	107
Price Testing	108
Selling Price	108
Premium Pricing	109
Premium Branding	110
Customer Demand	110
Discounting	111
Multiple Income Streams	112
CHAPTER 8 SELLING IN PERSON	**114**
Buyers and Sellers	114
Sales Skills	115
Arts and Crafts Fairs	115
Finding Suitable Events	116

Before The Event	118
On The Day	121
During The Event	121
After The Event	123
Commissioned Work	124

CHAPTER 9 SELLING ONLINE — 128
Purchasing Decisions	128
Sales Platforms	128
Marketplace Platforms	129
Hosted eCommerce	130
eCommerce Website	130
Online Payments	131
Conversion Funnels	134
Packaging and Postage	136

CHAPTER 10 MARKETING YOUR BUSINESS — 139
What is Marketing?	139
Advertising and Public Relations	139
AIDA	140
Interruption Marketing	141
Permission Marketing	142
Unique Selling Point	143
Unique Experience Point	144
Personality Types	145
Psychology and Behaviour	145
Branding	147
Social Interactions	149
Press Releases	149
Measuring Performance	151

CHAPTER 11 CONTENT MARKETING — 153
What is Content Marketing?	153
Content Creation and Acquisition	154
Website Content	157
Written Content	158
Writing a Blog	159

Newsletters	161
Visual Content	163
Photographic Content	164
Digital Photography	165
Video Content	166
Content Layout Design	167
CHAPTER 12 ORGANIC AND PAID SEARCH	**171**
Search Engines	171
Search Engine Optimisation	172
Keywords and Content	172
Meta Tags	173
Website Design	174
Personas	175
Backlinks	176
Paid Search	177
Analytics	179
Digital Marketing Agencies	180
CHAPTER 13 SOCIAL MEDIA	**183**
Social Media Strategy	183
Thought Leaders	184
Attracting a Following	187
Social Media and Email	188
Comparing Social Media Platforms	189
Facebook	191
Twitter	191
Google Plus	192
YouTube	192
LinkedIn	193
Pinterest	194
Instagram	195
CHAPTER 14 COURSES AND WORKSHOPS	**197**
Aptitude and Skills	197
Formal Education and Training	197
Attending a Course or Workshop	198

Running a Course or Workshop	200
Finding Students and Taking Bookings	201
Course or Workshop Venue	202
Class Size and Pricing	203
Equipment and Supplies	204
Food and Drink	205
Legal Matters	205
Class Planning	206
Teaching Classes	207
CHAPTER 15 ORGANISING CRAFT FAIRS	**209**
Craft Fairs	209
Event Finances	210
Insurance	211
Finding a Venue	212
Date and Time	213
Finding Stallholders	213
Event Marketing	214
Directional Signs	216
Before The Event	216
Event Day	217
After The Event	217
CLOSING THOUGHTS	**219**
ACKNOWLEDGEMENTS	**221**
ABOUT THE AUTHOR	**223**

INTRODUCTION

If you are considering running your own business, then you will probably have many questions about what is involved. I certainly did when I became self-employed. I was advised to develop an understanding of the many elements involved in setting up and growing a business, including tasks that when I was an employee would have been part of another persons job description. I also recall receiving advice regarding the importance of spending some time developing a greater sense of self-awareness and understanding what you really want in your life and work. Be prepared to find that the more you learn, the more you will realise how much you were previously unaware of and how much more there is still to learn. However, whilst running your own business can be hard work, when you are doing something that you love it can bring many rewards, including greater freedom to control your life and follow a path of your own choosing.

I am one of the founders of UKCraftFairs, which was inspired by our search for events, at which family and friends could exhibit and sell items that they had made. This led to the development of our website, where artists and makers can promote their work and find craft fairs, courses and exhibitions. We have also run our own craft fairs, enabling us to understand events from the perspective of organisers, exhibitors and visitors. Over the years we have met and worked with a wide range of creative people, from beginners to experienced professionals. This has provided us with a broad perspective and insight into what is involved in building a successful business and motivated me to write this book. Topics covered include the creative process, managing finances, customer relationships, pricing, sales and marketing. The book also explores social media, setting up your website, online search, managing business data and attending or organising craft workshops and craft fairs.

Although running your own business requires a wide a range of skills, you do not need to be an expert at everything. It is possible to start with limited resources and learn the skills that will enable you to achieve your goals. As your business grows, managing your time effectively and prioritising objectives in your life and work will help you to succeed. Having some understanding of the various roles required to run a business, can help you to make good decisions, regarding the tasks that you prefer to carry out yourself and those better outsourced to experienced professionals. I organised the content within these pages so that you can read the book from cover to cover at your own pace, or use it as a guide and easily find the information you want. Applying to your life and work, what you learn by reading this book, will help you to craft your own path to success.

CHAPTER 1 GETTING STARTED

Foundations of Success

Building a successful business requires planning, organisation, hard work and selling a product or service that can attract sufficient customer sales to cover your costs and generate a profit. What you are selling might be developed from a new idea or based upon improvements to something already available. As an artist or craft maker, your work might meet a practical need, but should also have aesthetic qualities that appeal to your clients sense of taste and style. In addition to having the necessary knowledge and skills to run a business, personal qualities can help you to succeed, such as creativity, self-awareness, social intelligence and confidence. A sense of purpose and clearly defined business objectives can help you to focus upon what needs to be done to achieve your goals. Being able to recognise opportunities and having the confidence to make good decisions enables you to adapt when needed. You should learn from both success and failure, knowing how and when to seek help or delegate tasks to other people, so that you can concentrate on the core essentials of your business.

Most artists and craft makers are self-employed and many of them will be working out of a studio or workshop, which might be located within their own home or a rented space. Reasons for wanting to work for themselves could include being free to develop their creative talents and skills, whilst exploring subjects of interest to them, without having to follow the instructions of an employer. They could also avoid spending time each day commuting to work or having to deal with office politics and organise a schedule that is suitable for their lifestyle or responsibilities, such as raising a family. Rather than having to do the same job each day, with a set routine and limited scope, running your own business will require you to take on a wide range of responsibilities. You are therefore less likely to experience boredom or feel that your abilities are not being challenged and allowed to grow. If your hard work eventually leads to great success, then you will benefit directly, rather than relying on an employer to recognise and reward your achievements.

Rather than creating work purely to earn money, artists and craft makers often want to earn money so that they have the time, resources and freedom to create their own work. However, it is important to be aware of issues that might cause a business to fail such as poor cash flow management, becoming dependent upon too few customers or spreading resources too thin and losing focus on the core product or service. Other risks include failing to properly comply with laws and regulations, not putting aside enough money to pay tax bills and having insufficient insurance to cover claims. Although success cannot be guaranteed, by managing your business effectively you should be able to avoid or minimise such dangers. If you are concerned about your ability to compete with other creative businesses, or the financial risk of self-employment, carry out market research, write a business plan, start small and grow at a rate that you are comfortable with. A bigger regret than starting your own business and failing, might be never trying and wondering if you could have succeeded.

Many people talk about wanting to start their own business, but they are often put off doing so by doubt in their own abilities and fear of failure. If such concerns are holding you back, then try to evaluate the viability of your business idea and acquire any additional knowledge, skills or resources that you need. Although success cannot be guaranteed, failure can teach you valuable lessons and might eventually help you to find your own path to success. If you have family responsibilities and are currently employed in a secure well paying job then you might decide that it is not worth the risk. In such a situation you could continue holding down a full time job, while you start a new business and only take the big step into self-employment after you have proved to yourself and your family that your business can succeed.

Ultimately though the decision of whether to set up your own business will depend upon your personal circumstances and the strength of your motivation to do so.

Understanding what is involved in setting up and running your own business, will help you to make informed decisions and reduce the risk that you will make basic mistakes. You might have decided to base your business around your work as an artist or craft maker and already posses the skills and experience needed to create items that people want to buy. If you have a passion for what you do, then that will give you a huge advantage compared to someone who is driven solely by financial gain. However, building a successful business will require a wide range of knowledge and skills in addition to your creative talents. It is therefore worthwhile investing time and effort into learning such skills, which will help you to develop a sound business plan. Although the way that you run your business might not be perfect, it should enable you to attract enough customers and generate a profit that is sufficient to meet your needs.

Starting Small

Many people self-fund their new business, rather than obtaining a bank loan or receiving outside financial support. Although this can present challenges when you are trying to get a product or service to market and attract your first customers, there are advantages to starting small and relying on your own resources. You will not be under pressure from investors to give them a quick return on their money or have to service a business related debt. Also you will retain control of your business and as an artist or craft maker you will be free to explore your creative ideas and look for customers who appreciate your work. Rather than trying to grow too quickly before you are ready, you will be able to focus on what needs to be done to establish a sustainable business. This could then can be scaled up as your business becomes more successful and you might decide to look for appropriate financial support to help your business grow and meet increasing demand.

Products and Services

Building a business around something that you enjoy doing and which brings you feelings of personal fulfilment can motivate you more than doing it only for money. However, you will still need to have a product or service that you can sell at a profit, find enough customers and generate sufficient turnover to remain in business. As an artist or craft maker you might already have sold your work, either online or in real life, perhaps to generate some additional income, or you could be considering making a hobby into a full time business. Based upon your skills and experience, you might already know what you are going to sell, where you are going to sell and how to attract customers. However, it is worthwhile considering what products or services could return the greatest profit and provide the best chance of building a successful business. Selling a clearly defined service or range of items will help you to focus your resources upon producing work of premium quality and make it easier to establish a strong brand identity for your business.

When a business brings a new product or service to market, there is a considerable investment of time and money involved. Therefore rather than risk losing money by failing to deliver what customers want or getting the pricing wrong, it is common for a business to begin by market testing with a few prototypes. The term minimum viable product (MVP) has been used to describe a version with basic features, that can be market tested with a sample of the target audience. Instead of trying to generate a profit from the prototypes, think of them as an investment in product and service testing. You could supply these test versions either at no charge or cost price to people you know and existing customers, whose judgement you trust. Based upon the feedback you receive, you could make changes and then market test again. Repeating this cycle should provide you with the information you need to develop premium products or services that customers want and at a price which they are prepared to pay, whilst leaving you with sufficient profit.

If you are going to be selling artwork or handmade crafts, then during the planning stage you could consider the subject matter, cost of materials and time required to create each item. As the amount of work you produce increases, you might be able to reduce costs by purchasing materials in larger volumes. Creating a series of related limited edition items, could attract the interest of people who enjoy collecting sets and could lead to additional sales as you make new pieces. Business owners could be offered handmade promotional items, perhaps carrying their logo and other forms of branding. Such items could be based upon existing designs or created to meet client specifications. Attaching personalised labels, with your business name and web address, to items that you sell, might attract repeat orders from existing customers and attract new clients, for example when people receive your work as a gift.

Visiting arts and crafts exhibitions, shops and fairs, might inspire and motivate you. In addition to providing an opportunity to network, you could get a feel for what people are buying and see how much they are paying. In addition to selling finished items, you could also put together craft kits containing the tools, materials and instructions that would enable someone to make a piece of work. The arts and crafts kits could be boxed, carry your business branding and be sold online or at events, to people who might be interested in taking up a new hobby. If you have excellent organisational skills and planning experience then you might decide to run your own arts and crafts events. You could also create commissioned work or run courses and workshops teaching creative skills to other people.

Becoming Self Employed

An individual who occasionally sells a few items would not generally be considered self-employed. However, if they are selling items on a regular basis or trading their skills for some form of payment then this could be classed as self-employment. For example, whilst being employed by someone else, you might have a hobby which you develop into a business during your spare time. If you are uncertain whether you could be classed as self-employed, you should seek advice, perhaps from an accountant or business advisor. You could also contact the relevant tax authorities, which if you are in the United Kingdom would be HM Revenue and Customs (HMRC) and if you are in the United States the Internal Revenue Service (IRS). They can advise you as to your status and if necessary what you must do to register your business and yourself as self-employed. You will also need to decide upon the structure and status of your business and should seek legal advice to ensure that you comply with the relevant legislation.

Sole Trader and Sole Proprietorship

When you begin running a business on your own, you will automatically be classed as a sole trader if you are in the United Kingdom and sole proprietorship if you are in the United States. With both, the business and the business owner are considered to be the same legal entity. This is the most common form of business and does not require you to go through the formal process of establishing a business structure. The business could be operated under your own name or one of your own choosing and without the need to consult co-owners, business decisions can usually be made quickly. The main disadvantage of this arrangement is that the business owner is personally liable for any debt that the business accumulates. They could also be viewed by potential clients and investors as less credible than more formal business entities. As a sole trader or sole proprietorship you will still be subject to the relevant laws of doing business and you must submit an individual tax return each year. You should seek legal advice to ensure that are aware of and abide by any and all regulations.

Business Partnership

If you decide to set up in business with one or more other people, you will be in a partnership and as with a sole trader or sole proprietorship, taxes would be payable by you as an individual. As partners you would be making business decisions together and in addition to sharing the profits, you would be jointly liable for any business debts. This would mean that if your other business partners were either unable or unwilling to pay their share of such a debt, then you could find yourself having to pay the total amount yourself. This requires a high level of trust between the partners and confidence that they can each be relied upon to meet their share of responsibility. Disagreements as to how the business should be run could emerge and it is therefore advisable to have a written partnership agreement, detailing rights and responsibilities. To ensure that you understand the implications and requirements of being in a business partnership, you should seek legal advice.

Limited Company and Limited Liability Company

When setting up your business you should consider how you want it to grow in the future and you might decide to establish a company with its own separate legal identity. In the United Kingdom this would take the form of a limited company (Ltd), whilst in the United States it would be a Limited Liability Company (LLC). Although there are some differences between them, they both issue privately held and traded shares and compared to sole trader or sole proprietorship will have greater credibility with clients and investors. One of the main benefits of a Ltd company (United Kingdom) or LLC (United States) is that the owners are protected from personal liability if the business is pursued by creditors for unpaid debts. You should ensure that you understand the advantages and disadvantages of running a Ltd company or LLC. Obtain legal advice to ensure that you comply with relevant laws and pay taxes as required in the jurisdiction where your business was formed and where you do business.

Limited Company in the United Kingdom

To set up a limited company in the United Kingdom, you must register it with Companies House. Registration of a new limited company can be done online or by post and although you could form a company yourself, you might prefer to seek professional advice about what is involved. The process is called incorporation and requires a company name and address, in addition to one or more directors and one or more shareholders. There are standard form templates available online, which you could use to ensure the information is entered correctly. After completing the necessary paperwork, such as a memorandum of association, articles of association, allocation of shares and their value, you will receive a Certificate of Incorporation, with the company number and the date it was formed. Within three months of being set up, a company must be registered for Corporation Tax, which UK companies are required to pay on their profits.

The directors of a UK limited company are legally responsible for the proper running of the company and they often, though not always, own shares. They must ensure that the company complies with the law, company accounts are filed and taxes paid, though they will often hire an accountant to manage much of this work. Companies are fined if they do not file the necessary paperwork on time or make payments late. Company directors must complete a personal self-assessment tax return each year and are typically paid a salary of an amount close to the personal allowance and receive dividends from company profits. You could visit the relevant UK government websites to learn more about setting up and running a limited company, along with the responsibilities of company directors. If you have any doubts or questions regarding your rights and responsibilities you should seek expert advice.

Limited Liability Company in the United States

The regulations involved in setting up a Limited Liability Company in the United States differ from state to state. There are certain basic steps involved and you can find information online regarding the particular requirements of the state where you intend forming your company. Having chosen a suitable business name, you will need to file articles of organisation, listing the name of the LLC, its members and their contact details. You can download the necessary form from your secretary of state's website. There will be a filing fee and some states charge annual taxes and annual fees. It is good practice to have a written agreement, recording each members roles, responsibilities, rights and the percentage of the business they own. Although you are not required by law to hire a lawyer, you could benefit from having a lawyer review your paperwork. They could also provide you with advice about legal matters you should be aware of when setting and running your own business.

Business Plan

The purpose of a business plan is to provide yourself and other people, such as a potential investor or bank manager, with an overview of your business ideas, goals and strategy. It can help you to create an organised structure for your thoughts, provide a path that you could follow, might help you to spot potential issues or opportunities and establish targets against which to measure progress. Before starting a new business it is advisable to write a business plan, though you should expect to update it over time as the business grows and adapts to changing conditions. Rather than worrying about details, or feeling restricted by what you write at this early stage, view it as an opportunity to take a step back and think about what you want to do and how you might achieve your goals. If you need advice regarding the writing of your business plan, you could speak to your accountant, an experienced business professional or your bank and you will find business plan templates online.

A typical business plan could begin with a front page that includes; a title, brief introduction, the author's name, business name, contact details and the date. This could be followed by a page listing the contents that will appear within the business plan. An executive summary could provide relevant background information on the people who will be running the business, along with a brief overview of your objectives and what each section of the business plan will cover. This could be followed by your vision statement and mission statement. Although your business might not begin to make a profit for some time and this can present practical difficulties, the plan should concentrate on building towards long term success. Whilst mass produced and commoditised products and services dominate the global economy, there is a growing appreciation of the philosophy and aesthetics of handmade arts and crafts. Most businesses in this sector are small, enabling you to compete with established brands and remain flexible, so that you can adapt your strategy when necessary to benefit from new opportunities.

The main sections of the business plan should go into greater detail and could provide supporting information, including suitable illustrations, graphs and tables of data. Sections might include a description of the product or service to be sold, the demand it will meet or niche it will fill, research carried out into the available market opportunities, who your customers will be and how demand will be met. There could also be reviews of existing competitors, a business model representing what the business does, funding and asset requirements, a sales and marketing strategy, pricing and financial projections, with expected turnover and profits for the months and years ahead. A cashflow forecast could be presented in the form of a spreadsheet, with a column for each month and a row for each expected cost or income source.

Market Research

When you are intending to set up a business, it is important that you carry out some market research, which involves the collection and analysis of relevant information about the potential customers for the product or service you are planning to sell. Having decided what type of business you want to run, you could begin by looking at existing businesses that already provide similar products or services. You could visit their websites, review their range of products or services, look at their social media activity and try to develop an understanding of the type of customers that they attract. The Internet is an excellent source of information, including government and business statistics that are within the public domain. Other sources of useful information include libraries, directories, professional associations and guilds. You could also ask people within your target audience to complete online or printed surveys, with questions designed to gather the information you are looking for. The type of data you need would include the size of your potential customer base, their location, demographics and buying habits.

Rather than trying to compete directly with existing businesses, you could look for opportunities to sell a niche product or service, if you can identify sufficient demand to support a profitable business. Alternatively you might be able to compete with established businesses by providing their customers with better quality products or services, running a more efficient operation and offering added value, such as superior customer service and a more personalised customer experience. When evaluating your business, you could carry out a SWOT analysis. This involves listing the Strengths, Weaknesses, Opportunities and Threats for your business and can help you to identify essential information that could impact upon the potential for your business and what you might need to do to ensure that it succeeds. As a result of your market research, you should be able to determine whether there is sufficient customer demand for the products or services that you are intending to sell and how your planned business could perform compared to the competition.

Mission Statement and Vision Statement

Whether you are considering starting a new business or already running a business, well defined mission and vision statements can be of great value. They each serve an important though different purpose and are often confused with each other, but when used to guide business strategy and planning can increase the chances of success. Some business owners put off developing their own mission statement and vision statements, because of the time and effort involved or doubts about their usefulness. However, either not having them or poorly defining them can result in inefficient use of resources, reduced brand consistency, increased costs and lost sales. Carrying out the research and analysis needed to develop effective statements for your own business provides you with an opportunity to think clearly about and express what you do and why, along with what you hope to achieve.

A mission statement can describe what your business does, identify your target audience and describe how you deliver a product or service. It should use the present tense and could refer to a period covering the next few years. Over time the mission statement can be updated, to reflect changing market conditions and new products or services. A well written mission statement can help both yourself, your customers and any employees understand the objectives and priorities of your business. This can lead to improved decision making, convert ideas into actions and provide perspective on how particular tasks contribute to delivering overall success. An example of a mission statement would be; to create handmade arts and crafts using traditional materials and techniques, for customers who appreciate premium quality unique items.

The vision statements for your business describe what you want to achieve over the long term, perhaps five or ten or more years into the future. They should establish an ideal to strive towards and inspire yourself, anyone else who works for the business and your customers. Although business strategies and short term objectives might change, a vision statement can be a consistent reference point, providing your business with a sense of direction, purpose and meaning. A well written vision statement can have an emotional appeal, transcending the practical day to day requirements of running a business and give people a shared ambition of wanting to achieve something together. An example of a vision statement would be; finding a fulfilling sense of purpose by creating work that inspires and brings joy to other people.

When developing mission and vision statements for your business, you should research the market that you will be serving. Ask potential customers what they look for in products or services that they buy and which you are intending to sell. This might include the use of online questionnaires or surveys carried out in real life, such as when attending arts and crafts fairs. Write statements that reflect your business priorities and engage with the preferences and values of your target audience. Whilst you will typically only have a single mission statement, you could write several vision statements. Take a broad approach, so that you explore a wide range of possible ideas and include essential information. Having written proposed mission and vision statements, you should seek feedback from a representative sample of people regarding how effective they think each will be, before deciding which to use.

Having written your mission and vision statements, you will need to decide how you are going to make use of them. Statements should be reflected in the way that you do business, the shaping of a strong consistent brand identity and messaging through all forms of communication. They could be included in website text, social media posts and printed on stationery or a wide variety of marketing materials. Inspiring mission and vision statements can provide you with clear goals, a path to follow and motivate you to overcome self-doubt and challenges that you might encounter. They can also attract other people to your work, who appreciate what you create and the philosophy of what you do, helping to make your business a success and enabling you to continue earning a living doing something that you love.

Business Name

When you know what product or service you are going to sell, have carried out market research and established your target audience, you will need to decide upon a suitable name for your business. The name you choose will help to create in the mind of your potential customers a sense of the identity of your business, so try to think of something that produces the first impression that you want to give. For example you could use your own name, focusing attention upon yourself as an artist or craft maker, or the name you choose could describe the work that you create and include keywords relating to your business. If possible, your business name should be available to register as a website domain name and with popular social networking platforms, so that you can use vanity URLs with the same name as your business. You should confirm that no existing business is using a confusingly similar name, ensure the name is not already trademarked and avoid using any potentially offensive or misleading wording.

Branding

You could think of a brand as the personality of a business and it is important that your business has a brand that will appeal to your potential customers. You want to be perceived as professional and reliable, projecting your creative talent and experience. In addition to the name of your business, important elements of branding include a well designed logo, a good strapline or slogan and an effective visual style, using an appropriate font and colour scheme. Your branding will represent your business across all forms of digital and print media, including stationery, packaging, leaflets, point of sale displays, website design and social media presence. Although you could do the work yourself, unless you are a skilled designer, you should consider employing the services of professionals to develop the branding for your business. The money invested in having a premium quality brand will help to instil confidence in your customers that they are paying for superior products or services. Branding which looks cheap or amateurish could put off potential customers, who might otherwise consider buying from you.

Work Space

When starting a business, among the first decisions that you will have to make is whether to base yourself at home or find an appropriate location elsewhere. Many artists and craft makers work out of a dedicated space within their home, whilst others prefer to rent a studio or workshop. The requirements of your business and the available budget will be factors in your decision, but it is essential that you create a good working environment. If you expect to be meeting clients, then you should also consider where you will be able to do so in comfort, without being disturbed. In addition to the necessary equipment, tools and materials for your art or craft, you will need adequate space within which you can store stock and carry out tasks such as packaging the items that you create. Although administrative tasks could be done on a laptop computer, you might need a dedicated office area where you can manage the various activities needed to run a well organised business, such as sales and marketing.

Converting a room within your home into a studio or workshop will have upfront costs, though in addition to saving money on rent, the business might also be able to contribute towards paying some bills and possibly bring tax benefits. Check your position regarding home insurance, taxes, possible health and safety issues and whether there are any legal restrictions relating to the type of work that you will be doing. When setting up your workspace, try to make it both efficient and conducive to creativity, perhaps by decorating it with some inspiring artwork. Not having to dress formally or endure a daily commute can be appealing to people who decide to work from home, but you will need to motivate yourself to get work done, despite the many possible distractions. For example you could set yourself fixed working hours, develop a routine and wear specific clothes, to get you in the right frame of mind each day when you are preparing to begin work.

For some people, such as parents raising a family, home working allows them to plan the hours that they work each day to suit their schedule. However, you should consider in what ways the arrangement could affect other people who share your home. If possible, try to keep your work space separate from your living space, even if this only involves a closed door with a do not disturb sign. You might decide to start your business at home, with the intention of renting a studio or workshop when sufficient profits are generated to cover the additional costs. Although such a move could initially affect your profitability, it might result in you being more productive and selling more work. For example you should be able to more clearly separate home and work, establish a defined routine and concentrate on your work with fewer distractions. Clients might also perceive you as being more professional, if you are able to meet with them in a business setting rather than your own home.

Rather than negotiating a long lease, you might prefer to look for space that can be rented on a monthly basis. Depending upon the nature of your work, you could rent a serviced office, which might include many of the costs associated with having your own office. A serviced office could also be in a convenient location, have office equipment already in place and offer shared resources such as support staff and receptionists. If you want a retail outlet, then you could look for a shop that is available on a short lease. During recent years coworking spaces have become popular with startups, the self-employed and freelance workers, such as technology professionals, writers and designers. The spaces are typically designed to create a relaxed informal atmosphere and encourage collaboration between the people working there. They can provide a break from the home working environment and support the growth of business communities. In addition to networking opportunities, coworking spaces typically offer shared resources and could allow an artist or craft maker to focus on business related tasks such as administration, sales and marketing, away from their studio or workshop.

Business Insurance

As a business owner, you should have insurance providing adequate cover for claims that might result from damage or injury caused by your business and the products or services that it supplies. Even if your are running a small business, you should look for policies that will cover costs such as legal expenses and compensation that might be awarded. Product liability insurance provides cover for compensation due to injury or damage caused by products that you supply, such as works of art or handmade crafts that you create. You will need to insure your company for claims made due to personal injury or damage to property caused by your business. In the United Kingdom this type of insurance is called public liability insurance and in the United States it is called general liability insurance. A business with employees, will also need to have employers liability insurance to cover for claims such as employee related illness or injury.

Business insurance might not be available from your home insurance provider and some insurers might not cover artists or craft makers. When looking for an insurance provider, you could either compare their quotes yourself or seek the assistance of an insurance broker who has experience negotiating on behalf of the type of business that you run. The cost of insurance will depend upon factors such as the size and location of your business, the level of cover required, the nature of your business and any inherent risks associated with the type of business that you are running. Before choosing an insurance provider, you should read the small print to ensure that you understand exactly what is covered by any policy you are considering. You should be aware of any exclusions that apply to the insurance policy that you choose. To ensure that you obtain the most appropriate insurance for your business, you should seek independent professional advice.

Health and Safety

Every business must comply with laws that are intended to protect customers, employees and the general public. In the United Kingdom, the Health and Safety at Work Act covers regulations relating to the responsibilities of employers and employees to ensure a safe working environment. The Foods Standards Agency (FSA) is responsible for food safety and hygiene and catering businesses should be visited by local authority inspectors, who are responsible for ensuring that food and food preparation areas meet the required standards. To find information about certificates that businesses trading in the UK will need, along with associated fees, you could visit the

Health and Safety Executive (HSE) website and contact relevant trade bodies or local authorities. Having the appropriate documentation for your business, which proves that you are in compliance with the relevant legislation, might also have implications for your insurance cover.

Within the United States, the Occupational Safety and Health Act regulates laws relating to the provision of a safe working environment. There are also regulations relating to the provision of goods and services, such as food to be sold to the public, and you should be aware of the laws that apply in the states where you will be doing business. For example, there could be requirements relating to the equipment or materials that you use in your work, such as machinery run within a studio or workshop, or equipment used in demonstrations of your craft at a craft fair. It is the business owners responsibility to ensure that they are aware of any legislation relating to the business that they run, along with recommendations and best practice. To ensure that your business is in compliance with the relevant legislation, you could look for information online, contact the appropriate authorities and seek independent professional advice.

Data Security

It is important that you put processes and systems in place that will safeguard your personal and business data, along with the information of individuals or organisations that you do business with. For example, customer data that is recorded so as to deliver a product or service should be stored securely and not used inappropriately. Particular care should be taken to protect information that could be used to identify an individual. Although the United States does not have comprehensive legislation covering data protection, there are laws relating to certain types of information, such as in the health and finance sectors. In the United Kingdom, data protection is regulated by the Information Commissioner's Office (ICO). From May 25th 2018, the General Data Protection Regulation (GDPR) provides a framework for data protection laws across the European Union. To learn more about compliance with legislation where you are doing business, you could contact the relevant authorities or visit their website.

To reduce the risk of becoming a victim of deception or fraud, whether online or in real life, only share information with individuals or organisations that you trust. Verify that people who contact you are who they claim to be and do not provide information they are requesting unless you believe there is a good reason to do so. Carry out due diligence, such as researching suppliers of a product or service that you are offered and look online for genuine comments from their existing customers. Rather than responding to telephone calls or emails claiming to be from a particular organisation, obtain the correct contact details from a trusted source and then communicate directly with that organisation to discuss the matter further. Ensure that you install security updates for any devices that you use, such as desktop or laptop computers, tablets or mobile phones and verify the safety of software before you download it.

Personal Skills and Resources

In addition to possessing the skills needed to provide the products or services that your business will sell and the ability to run a business, there are personal qualities and resources that could help you to succeed. Strategic thinking will allow you to define objectives and plan how you are going to achieve them, whilst good time management will enable you to prioritise and complete tasks efficiently. Good physical and mental health will help you to maintain the stamina required to work the long hours typically needed to start, run and grow your own business, along with the resilience to cope with the many challenges involved. A positive outlook on life can help you to find the confidence needed to overcome setbacks. However, the ability to be honest about strengths and weaknesses within yourself and others is also important, as is learning from mistakes. Good social skills can make it easier to work with, listen to, understand and learn from other people, helping you to engage effectively with customers and make sales.

Technology can enable you to more efficiently and securely manage business information and communications, even though you might have only a mobile phone and a computer, running appropriate software, linked to peripherals such as a printer and scanner. However, you should remember that technology is merely a useful tool and it should not distract you from the core activities involved in running your business. You should establish a comfortable work space, where you can be well organised, enabling you to quickly and easily end work each day and be ready to start again the following day. Without being reckless or incompetent, either with your own or other people's investment of time and money, be prepared to take calculated risks. Rather than being afraid to fail you should look for new opportunities, learn from failure and try again. Many businesses have been started by people who overcame earlier failures before finding a path to success.

When you work for someone else, you will probably have a clearly defined role, requiring specific skills. However, running your own business will require you to develop a wide range of skills, in addition to those needed to create your work, provide services or organise events, such as courses, workshops or craft fairs. For some specialist activities it is sensible to hire experienced professionals, who can complete tasks more quickly and to a higher standard than you could. For example you might employ the services of specialists to design your logo and branding, develop your website, manage your business accounts and handle legal matters. However, it can be beneficial learning about areas such as marketing, pricing, sales, customer service, social media, finance and law. Doing so could help you to better understand what to expect from the professionals that you hire and ensure that they provide a good quality service, or you could save money by taking on some of the work yourself.

Employing Other People

As a business owner, it is essential that you focus sufficient time and energy on delivering your core product or service and maintain the quality your customers expect. Therefore even though you might know how to complete particular time consuming tasks, such as administration, finding new customer leads and the packaging of items for delivery, you might decide to hire someone to do this work. However, you should think carefully about the costs involved in taking on employees and decide whether the extra income you will be able to generate through the business due to increased sales will make it cost effective. You could calculate an hourly monetary value for the work that you do, determine how much extra time you would be able to devote to your work and then compare this to the additional costs. Before taking on the financial and legal responsibilities involved in employing staff, you could hire somebody on a temporary basis, perhaps to help during seasonal increases in workload. There are also many online services, offering to manage a wide variety of tasks.

When starting your own business you might hire professional services to help with areas such as accountancy, branding, marketing or sales. These people will likely be self-employed and paid on the basis of the work they do, as and when required. However, your business could grow to the point where an increasing workload makes it cost effective to employ someone either part time or full time. Unless you have a family member or friend who is able and willing to take on the role, then you will need to find suitable candidates, perhaps by advertising online or within suitable publications. You will then need to interview applicants, to find a person with the necessary skills and experience, who you are confident you can trust and work well with. When employing staff, you must verify their legal right to work, ensure that the necessary paperwork is submitted for taxation purposes and obtain relevant insurance cover. You will also need to pay employees no less than minimum wage, provide them with a written statement of the terms of employment and comply with employment legislation.

Team Building

If your business reaches the stage at which you begin to employ a team of people, then look for those with skills that complement each other. This will help to ensure that your business has the diverse range of skills required to make the most of opportunities to deliver products and services that your customers will want. When hiring new employees, you could introduce them to current team members and get feedback to help you evaluate their suitability for the role. Going purely on first impressions could cause you to hire someone who looks good on paper, whilst missing out on a person who though less qualified or lacking as much experience might work harder, contribute more and deliver better results. Create a working environment that encourages creativity and initiative, supports trust and cooperation between team members, inspires confidence in each others abilities and provides good management leadership, with clear mission and vision statements.

Business Organisations and Networks

When you are running your own business you might not have a lot of spare time, but the benefits of attending business networking events can make them worthwhile. It is true to say that people prefer to do business with other people who they know and like. However, do not think of a business network as a place for you to make direct sales. You should instead consider it to be somewhere that you can build mutually beneficial relationships with other business owners, which might lead to future opportunities. You could share your expertise with people you meet, who might appreciate the help that you give them and recommend your services to people that they know. Events might be held at which guest speakers talk about important legislation and issues could arise of concern to local business owners, requiring joint action. You could ask people that you know about business networks that they are members of, search online for networking groups in your area, or look for online networks, where you might find advice and support.

In many towns and cities there are business networks, that provide an opportunity for people running their own business to meet, share ideas and find useful resources. There can also be psychological benefits to attending business networking events, as self-employment can lead to feelings of isolation and loneliness. You might miss the social interaction of being in a busy workplace, particularly if you are working from home, and having the chance to meet other people could be a welcome change. It is natural to feel a little nervous or shy when attending an event and meeting new people, so try to relax and realise that most people understand this and will try to make you feel welcome and involved. Whilst some business forums and networks might be free to join, others could have a membership fee to cover running costs. They might hold regular events within a venue such as a community centre or business centre, perhaps for a few hours each week or month.

There might be a professional or trade association that you could join, allowing you to meet other people in your line of work, enabling you to compare experiences and seek advice. Rotary clubs exist across the world, bringing together people from a diverse range of backgrounds, to support service that is of benefit to society. You could join your local chamber of commerce, where you will find people from many different professions and businesses. Regular attendance and being an active contributor could raise your profile, increase awareness of your business among other members and lead to opportunities that might help your business to grow. If you want to join a local group for artists, craft makers or designers, but are unable to find one, then you could set up your own and invite others to join. The Crafts Council promotes the development of contemporary crafts in the United Kingdom and provides resources intended to support craft makers, artists and designers. The American Craft Council (ACC) has a similar role in the United States, where it provides resources and runs events that encourage the growth of art, craft and design.

CHAPTER 2 MANAGING YOUR FINANCES

Business Finances

Each year thousands of new businesses are formed and whilst many of them go on to be successful, others fail. Some businesses misjudge the market and are unable to find enough customers, whilst others enjoy a period of growth, but are then overtaken by changing tastes or technology. However, the most common cause of business failure is financial difficulties due to cash flow problems. Even a business selling excellent products or services to satisfied customers could cease trading, if they run out of money and are unable to meet outstanding bills. As an artist or craft maker you might prefer to focus your energies on creative work, rather than finance and accounting. However, the success of your business will depend upon good money management. It is therefore important that you remain aware of the financial situation of your business at all times and that you are able to manage your cash flow effectively.

Hiring the services of a good accountant should help you to avoid some of the potential financial pitfalls that you might encounter when running a business. Paying a professional to do some of the necessary paperwork will also leave you more time to focus on the core activities of your business and their advice could save you more money than you pay them. There should be processes in place to manage payments associated with the running of your business and accurate records kept of the money coming into and going out of your business. Also ensure there are sufficient funds set aside to cover any bills that you will need to pay. Not doing these things could mean that even with healthy sales, you might not notice if overall costs exceed earnings and your business could fail. Maintaining control of your finances could help your business to survive changing economic conditions by enabling you to adapt as required.

Including within your business plan relevant costs and the time scale involved for each stage of setting up and running your business could help you to avoid unexpected expenses or delays. Good time management and applying sound project management principles, such as completing tasks in an appropriate sequence, can reduce the risk of resources being used inefficiently and wasted. Building a profitable business means earning more money than you spend, so that you can cover the running costs and be left with a profit. You should ensure that you understand how your business is performing and it is useful therefore to be aware of some relevant terminology. The terms turnover or revenue can be used to refer to the total amount of income that a business generates. Gross profit is the amount left after the direct costs of the product or service that you are selling have been deducted. Net profit is the amount remaining after all other costs have been paid for, such as marketing, administration and tax.

Business Bank Account

Many people enjoy creating artwork and handmade craft items as a hobby and they might decide to sell some of their work at a location such as a craft fair or store or online. Initially relatively small sums of money could be involved and the artist or maker might trade under their own name, receiving and making payments through their personal bank account. However, such an arrangement will become difficult to manage if the volume of sales grows to the point where it begins to represent a real business rather than a hobby. Under such circumstances you should separate personal and business finances, by setting up an account to be used for business banking. Although a small business could be run as a sole trader or sole proprietorship, you might decide to set up a private limited company or limited liability company, which will need its own bank account.

Having a business bank account will enable you to make and receive payments under the name of your business, rather than your own name. This will look more professional to your clients and you should be given a cheque book and credit or debit cards in the name of your business. When deciding where to set up your business account you should compare what each bank offers, as some might include benefits for small business owners, such as an introductory period of free banking. You could also seek advice from other business owners, based upon their experiences. Consider costs such as monthly fees and transactional fees, and choose an account that you think will be suitable for your business, for example whether most of your customers pay in person using cash or if you trade mainly online.

When opening a business bank account, you will be asked to supply proof of your identity, the name and nature of your business and, depending upon the type of business, relevant documents relating to its legal status. It is also possible that you would be asked to show a business plan, demonstrating that your business is viable. Before deciding where to bank, you could begin by carrying out research online, then visit branches of some local banks and ask to speak to someone about opening an account. Although you might not be able to meet a traditional bank manager, you might want there to be people available who you can speak to either in person or over the telephone, such as members of the business banking team. If you will be banking mainly online, then compare the quality of the online services that each bank provides. However, regardless of the bank you choose, ensure that your account is managed efficiently, monitor the balance and try to avoid unnecessary charges being applied.

Startup Finance

Although financing the startup stage of a business using your own savings or earnings from another job would give you greater control, you might need to seek additional support. You could decide to take out a loan, perhaps borrowing from family or friends, though you should ensure that you will be able to repay the debt or risk damaging important personal relationships. Arranging a bank loan might be difficult, though a good business plan should help and the bank will require adequate collateral, such as property or other assets. When borrowing money, you should ensure that the amount is sufficient to meet your needs, without being more than is required, as you will be making loan repayments with interest, which will impact your finances. Try to manage your finances effectively, in order to reduce the risk of incurring overdraft fees and so as to maintain a good credit score. Possible alternative funding options could include crowd funding, peer to peer lending or angel investors, who will look for credibility and the potential for a good return on their investment. Government backed loans might also be available to start a small businesses or to help it grow.

Startup Costs

When starting a new business, the available finances will probably be limited and your time taken up with many demands. However, you will need sufficient resources to create and market a product or service, cover daily running costs and eventually pay yourself an income. Lack of money could make it difficult to sustain your business, until sales generate sufficient revenue to break even and begin making a profit. Managing your finances sensibly, minimising debt and not wasting resources will increase the chances of success. Therefore you should seek ways of reducing costs and improving cash flow, by for example negotiating effectively with suppliers, arranging good payment terms and either hiring equipment or purchasing second hand rather than brand new. You should also look for opportunities to benefit from economies of scale as your business grows. Before you begin trading you should calculate how much money will be required and include this within your business plan. Although your figures are likely to be estimates, they should be based upon realistic data and you should be aware of the fixed and variable costs that you are likely to encounter.

Fixed Costs

Costs that remain the same regardless of the volume of items produced are called fixed costs, for example tools, equipment, company vehicles, insurance, training courses and staff wages, if you employ people. Other fixed costs could include those involved in the formation of your business, costs associated with a trademark or patent and professional fees, such as marketing, financial and legal services. Unless you are working from home or another property that you already own, your largest expense will probably be for suitable premises from which to run your business. Rather than taking on a commercial mortgage, you will likely be renting from a landlord, who in addition to an upfront deposit could require payment of a service charge. You might also have to cover the cost of refitting and decorating the premises before it is a safe, secure and comfortable place in which to work.

Variable Costs

Costs that increase or decrease according to the volume of items produced are called variable costs. Variable costs might include materials, packaging and shipping. A business could have other variable costs, for example if people employed by the business are paid for each item that they make or salespeople are paid commission on each completed sale. Some costs, such as utility bills, could be either fixed or variable. Although some other fixed costs might also vary, they are not typically included within the costs directly associated with the production of what is being sold.

Managing Cash Flow

Cash flow is the changing amount of money available within a business on a day to day basis. Whilst there might be a healthy profit when viewed on an annual basis, the realities of running a business mean that most will experience ups and downs. For example one month you could be purchasing new tools or materials, whilst another month you might be receiving payment for a completed piece of work. Also there could be periods of poor sales, due to seasonal factors and economic cycles or additional costs, such as unexpected bills or an increase in the cost of raw materials. However, a business must always have sufficient funds available to cover running costs and this requires good cash flow management, to ensure that at no time do you find yourself in the position of being unable to meet essential payments. You should therefore ensure that you manage debts and costs effectively and generate sufficient profits to provide the business with a reserve that can be set aside to survive the proverbial rainy days.

Find a convenient and reliable way of keeping track of the financial state of your business. Making and receiving payments through one business bank account will help you to see how your business is performing financially. Recording relevant data within a spreadsheet will provide an overview of your business finances, helping you to predict income and spending on a monthly, quarterly and annual basis. A single spreadsheet could represent a year, with expected costs or sources of income entered into separate rows and a column provided for each month. The recording of day to day financial transactions of a business is called bookkeeping. Although you could hire a bookkeeper to do this work, you might prefer to do it yourself, either using a suitable spreadsheet template or dedicated bookkeeping software, which you will probably find easier to use. You should be able to import data from your bank account into a bookkeeping package, saving time and reducing the risk of errors. Relevant information could then be exported in a format that you can send to your accountant when required.

Set aside enough money to cover regular outgoings, so that you can pay for them regardless of whether revenues rise or fall from month to month. Although you might be able to reduce expenditure in some areas, for example more cost effective advertising or more competitively priced materials, other regular costs will have to be met, such as utility bills, rent and insurance. To ensure that you have the funds available to pay tax bills on time, you could put the money into a separate savings account. Keep records of your spending and speak to your accountant about what you can claim as business expenses. Arranging monthly payments when making major purchases could spread out the cost, rather than having a huge impact on short term cash flow. If you are ordering materials in sufficient quantity, then you might be able to arrange improved terms with suppliers. However, you should ensure that you pay outstanding bills in full and on time, to maintain good working relations with your suppliers and avoid any penalties, for example you might have agreed to pay within thirty days.

When you are selling a finished product, such as a piece of artwork or handmade crafts, payment will typically be made upon delivery. Purchasing the materials for your art or craft in bulk could reduce per unit costs. However, you should only buy what you will need to meet expected demand for your work, so as to reduce the amount of money tied up in unused stock. By contrast if you are working on a commission you will typically provide a quote and arrange terms of payment. You should request a partial payment upfront and artists will often ask for between thirty and fifty percent before they commence work. This should cover your upfront costs, such as materials and reduce the risks of non payment. You can then invoice the client for the outstanding amount upon delivery of the finished item. However, the cash flow situation of a client might cause them to delay their payment to you. Therefore, before taking on a commission, you should consider the potential impact upon your business of late or non payment and preferably work for clients who you are confident will pay on time for the work done.

Taxes in the United Kingdom

In the United Kingdom, HM Revenue and Customs (HMRC) is responsible for collecting taxes. Whether you become self-employed as a sole trader, in a partnership or set up a limited company, HMRC must be informed, to ensure that you pay the correct amount of tax and national insurance. Registration can be done online and although you could manage your dealings with HMRC yourself, you might prefer to authorise your accountant to do so on your behalf. After the end of each tax year, a self-assessment tax return showing any salary or dividends you have received must be sent to HMRC, either by post or online. Income tax owed is calculated based upon reported income and you will be required to pay that amount by the due date. Regarding PAYE (pay as you earn), your accountant can set up the company payroll, so that tax and national insurance are deducted at source from salaries paid to employees and then paid to HMRC, quarterly or monthly.

As a sole trader you will be able to keep the profits earned by your business, after paying tax, national insurance and VAT, if your turnover is above the registration threshold. Unlike business partnerships in England, Wales and Northern Ireland, partnerships in Scotland have their own separate legal identity and are referred to as a firm. A limited company will pay its own taxes and profits will belong to the company, not the directors or shareholders. If you are a company director, then the business could pay you a salary and dividends, an arrangement that can have tax benefits, which your accountant should be able to advise you about. If you intend to buy or sell goods or services in other countries, then you should be aware of your position regarding taxation and if necessary seek independent expert advice.

In the United Kingdom value added tax (VAT) is charged on a wide range of goods and services, although some are exempt. A business expecting turnover to exceed the current VAT registration threshold during a twelve month period must become VAT registered and they will receive a VAT registration number. Subsequently the business must include VAT in the price of products or services that they sell and they will also be able to reclaim VAT paid on products or services they purchase. The business must maintain accurate accounts, retaining invoices and receipts, and every three months send a VAT return to HMRC. In effect the business is collecting VAT on behalf of HMRC and must pay them the amount owed by the due date, or be fined. Some businesses decide to become VAT registered even if their turnover is below the threshold. This might be because of the increased credibility with customers and other business owners, or because they want to reclaim VAT paid on their purchases.

Businesses with a turnover within a specific amount above the VAT registration threshold have the option to register for the Flat Rate Scheme. HMRC introduced the Flat Rate Scheme to simplify the administrative process for smaller businesses and in some circumstances it can reduce the amount they pay, although the business would no longer be able to claim back VAT on purchases. Such an arrangement might benefit a business that claims back only a small amount of VAT. To learn more, so that you can decide what is most appropriate for your business, speak to your accountant, visit the HMRC website or ring their telephone helpline.

Limited companies in the United Kingdom must register for corporation tax with HMRC and pay corporation tax on profits. The company must retain records of income and spending so that the amount owed can be calculated. The relevant paper and electronic records of business related financial transactions will be needed either by yourself or your accountant when managing the business accounts. Such records must be kept for five years if you are a sole trader and six years if you run a limited company. If HMRC notifies you that they will be auditing your business, then you would need to be able to provide them with the relevant records. When you are setting up and running your own business, dealing with HMRC can be intimidating and if you are unclear about any aspect of taxation you should speak to your accountant or contact HMRC.

Taxes in the United States

In the United States, self-employed people must normally file an annual tax return and pay both income tax and self-employment tax. Whether an individual would be considered self-employed will depend upon a number of factors, and if they are unsure of their status they should seek professional advice. The type of business entity will determine the income tax return forms that must be filed. For example, sole proprietorship, partnership, Limited Liability Company (LLC) or Corporation, will each have requirements. Many sole proprietors use their Social Security Number (SSN) when reporting their income to the Internal Revenue Service (IRS). However, an Employer Identification Number (EIN), which can also be known as a Federal Identification Number, will under some circumstances be required to identify a business entity. For example an EIN would be required when a business hires employees, or forms a partnership, Limited Liability Company, or corporation. A business owner with employees will have certain tax responsibilities and they should ensure that they are aware of what is required of them.

Unlike a corporation, an LLC in the United States is not a separate tax entity, but is instead a pass-through entity, which means that profits and losses pass through the business to the owners of the LLC, who are called members. As with individuals in a partnership or sole proprietorship, these members are not employees of the business, but self-employed business owners and they must report this information on the personal tax returns that they file with the IRS. There could be circumstances in which a person not resident in the United States, but who generates income from business activities in the United States, might be required to file a tax return. To ensure that they comply with the relevant legislation, an individual should seek appropriate legal and tax advice from a suitably qualified professional, who is familiar with the details of their circumstances.

Some business owners decide to form a corporation, which differs in a number of important ways from an LLC. For example, a corporation is a separate business entity and corporations pay taxes on their profits. Corporations will have a board of directors and a corporation can pay dividends to the business owners, who report such earnings on their personal tax return. To find information about payment of taxes, individuals could visit the IRS website or contact an IRS office. Business owners should be aware of any state taxes that need to be paid and understand their position regarding sales tax in the states where they do business. To receive advice regarding the advantages and disadvantages of each form of business, what is involved in changing the status of a business and compliance with relevant tax legislation, business owners should consult a suitably qualified adviser, who has the necessary experience.

CHAPTER 3 LIFE AND WORK

Your Ideal Job or Business

Do you enjoy your work? Does what you do give you such a deep sense of achievement and connection to other people and the world around you that you never want to retire? Would you continue with your work, which feels more like your life purpose or vocation, even if you became wealthy and could choose to never work another day in your life? Have you reached such a level of expertise in your chosen profession, trade, art or craft that you are considered by your peers to posses a remarkable natural talent? If your answer to these questions is yes, then you are very fortunate, as you are probably already doing work that suits your aptitude and aspirations. If your answer to these questions is no, then it might be time to consider changing your job, rethinking the direction your business is taking or starting a new business.

If you are planning to start you own business, you might have a clear idea of what you want to do, particularly if it is based upon skills and experience that you already possess. For example you might want to turn a hobby into a business, selling work that you have created. When working for someone else, the demands of your job could mean that you will struggle to develop a career path which closely matches your interests and aptitude. By contrast if you decide to become self-employed, you have the opportunity to think carefully about what you want to do and find a way to earn a living which brings you both personal fulfilment and a way of paying the bills. It is worthwhile taking the time you need to consider what you enjoy doing, what you are good at and what you want to achieve. Ask yourself what your perfect job would be and what skills and experience they would require. Find something that you would be sufficiently motivated by to devote the time and effort needed to succeed. Then take the actions in your life that are necessary to get there.

Building a business based upon something you enjoy doing and that you are good at will give it a greater chance of being successful, provided you can develop a viable business around it. For example people involved in arts and crafts tend to be drawn to it because they enjoy the creative process of making something and their ambition might be to earn a living doing work they have a passion for. If you are uncertain what your ideal business might be or in what direction to develop your skills, so as to be in accordance with your interests and aptitude, you could carry out a SWOT analysis of your life and work. This could help you to identify any strengths, weaknesses, opportunities or threats that might be relevant to the path you decide to follow.

Write down or enter into a spreadsheet a list of the things that you are good at and enjoy doing and those things that you dislike doing or find difficult. Record activities you choose to do in your spare time, recall subjects you liked or disliked from your school days and list your existing skills or those you would like to learn. Write down your strengths and weaknesses, such as your physical health, social support network, relevant knowledge and skills, experience, business related contacts, problem solving or analytical skills, creativity, financial resources and tools or equipment that you own. Looking at your SWOT analysis could help to highlight a suitable direction for your business and any additional assistance or resources that might be needed.

If the business that you want to start requires you to acquire new skills, then look realistically at the time and cost involved. If you are planning to base your business upon your existing skills, then you might want to find a niche product or service that you can offer. Entering relevant terms into a search engine and analysing the results, could help you to identify business opportunities. Visiting websites that sell products or services similar to those that you will be offering could give you some idea of what people are already buying and how much they are paying. Reading customer reviews and engaging on social media could help you to identify unmet demand for a product or service. Seek inspiration by brainstorming and through creative thinking, to find ways in which the products and services that you are familiar with might be improved upon and how you could differentiate what you are selling from what is already available.

Education and Work

It has long been thought that people such as Picasso and Shakespeare possessed an inborn genius beyond the vast majority of humanity. However, unlikely though it might seem, there is a growing belief that we might all have the potential to develop exceptional abilities, by devoting sufficient quality time to an activity which suits our interests and aptitude. Yet whilst some people go through the traditional educational system achieving academic success, others struggle. When they go out into the world of work, some people are well prepared to begin building their careers, whilst others find it more difficult. Why is this and why do some of those who struggled at school, find success in their chosen occupation, whilst others with excellent qualifications fail to find a fulfilling career?

We can complete years of study and training to prepare us for jobs in which we lack an active interest. Initially youthful optimism and busy social lives can mask feelings of having chosen the wrong path. Some people spend many of the best years of their life clock watching, looking forward to evenings, weekends and holidays. Later this can make it more difficult to find and keep a job. People following supposedly safe career paths, which are not suited to them, could miss out on opportunities and promotions to others who are more motivated, skilled and ambitious. Some who choose an occupation unsuited to them, because it promises wealth and fame or to please other people, might find themselves losing interest in their work and longing for something more fulfilling.

The idea of finding fulfilment through your work might sound irrelevant and even self-indulgent, when millions of people are competing against each other to find and hold on to a decent paying job. However, in a world of rapidly advancing technology and lack of job security, there could be considerable risk for anyone not taking steps to better match their interests and occupation, as this could lead to regrets, setbacks and failure. After working at an unsuitable job for ten or twenty years, people can find their careers stagnate, as they are overtaken or replaced by younger more eager or just cheaper workers and they could be confronted by the challenges of diminishing employment opportunities.

People who choose a career path well suited to them, will happily devote extra time and energy to developing superior skills and talents. Engrossed in their work, time seems to fly by as they develop an increasingly deep understanding and intuition for what they do. They become difficult to replace in their chosen line of work, as over the years of focused practice their abilities exceed their less motivated peers. As they progress, acquiring new knowledge and skills they are in a better position to find suitable work, build a successful career, create their own employment opportunities or start their own business.

Social Intelligence

Humans are the most social and political animals on the planet and one of our great strengths as a species is our ability to work effectively together to solve complex problems. We posses the capacity to have insight into each others inner thoughts, feelings and motivations through empathy, which enables us to more effectively navigate the social complexities of life and work. This requires an understanding of the concerns, drives and perspectives of other people, in our relationships with colleagues and clients, as well as family and friends. Social intelligence is therefore an important skill for those running a business, and will be used for example when finding clients and negotiating sales.

Traditionally we have as a society focused primarily on academic performance and IQ (Intelligence Quotient), believing them to be the primary indicators of future success in life and work. However, there is growing evidence that social intelligence and good communication skills play an equal and perhaps even greater role in how well someone will do in life. This is reflected in the old saying that achieving success is not just about what you know, but who you know. Therefore having a healthy network of people around you including family, friends and colleagues can help you in your career and in running your own business. Some people are born into circumstances which give them a head start in this respect, such as when benefiting from the old school tie. However, in the modern world it can be difficult to maintain and develop genuine friendships and mutually supportive relationships with other people.

Some individuals seem to have natural charm, which draws other people to them. Through an understanding of the needs and motivations of others, such people are able to build their own supportive networks of family, friends, colleagues and clients. However, many of us are uncomfortable in social situations and struggle to develop such support networks. To an extent our personality type will influence our behaviour and an extrovert will generally find socialising easier than an introvert. However, if you find yourself isolated, which can be a common problem for the self-employed, try taking the time to find people with whom you share common interests. For example you could do volunteer work, join a local business networking group or attend events related to your interests. Taking up a hobby or sport, could help to widen your social circle in addition to bringing potential health benefits. Developing such relationships could help to improve your quality of life and the prospects of success in your business, as you begin to better understand other people and engage more effectively with them.

For those working as an artist or craft maker, the ability to understand other people and put yourself in their place is an important part of creating work that will resonate with others. You might have heard great musicians saying that their instrument feels like it is a part of them when they play, this is an example of our capacity to relate ourselves not just to other people, but also animals, plants and inanimate objects, such as the tools of our trade. This tendency for people to relate human characteristics to the animals, plants or objects in the world around them led ancient cultures to worship spirit animals and create art such as the Paleolithic Lascaux cave paintings. It also produced within our minds the deities found in classical mythology and led to the writing of literary works such as Aesop's Fables.

There is a romantic image of artists working alone in their studio, misunderstood by those around them. However, if you are a talented artist creating great work but no one else ever sees your paintings or sculptures then you could die in poverty and obscurity. By contrast someone less talented than you but with better social skills might attract clients, be offered exhibition space and become a celebrated artist. For example if you are a maker of arts and crafts, when attending a craft fair you are more likely to sell your work if you smile and engage effectively with potential clients. Some well established individuals might prefer to let their work speak for itself, but you are more likely to find success if you have developed good social skills, such as looking for buying signals when selling your work.

Try not to become overly self-conscious and avoid fake sincerity, as socially intelligent people will realise that you are not being genuine and they will be less likely to trust you or want to be around you. Focusing too much on your own inner thoughts and fears will also be counter productive, as you risk missing out on the many subtle cues from other people. Try instead to silence your internal dialogue, watch other people and listen to what they are saying. Empathise with them, which can help you to better understand their perspective, motivations and true intentions. The growth of social media means also learning how you can best use it to promote your work and more effectively communicate with colleagues and clients.

Emotional Intelligence

Whilst social intelligence focuses on our behaviour and being aware of how we manage our relationships with other people, emotional intelligence is more about your level of self-awareness regarding your true feelings and those of others. Emotional intelligence enables us to have respect for our own needs and those of other people, bringing with it empathy, sympathy, tolerance and the ability to forgive yourself and others. Stress can result from being unable to cope with challenging social and emotional situations, which can undermine your relationships and lead to poorer health. Learning how to better understand and manage your emotions, so that you react appropriately to a given situation can help to reduce stress, improving your personal and business relationships. You will also feel a greater sense of well being and have more energy to focus on your work when needed.

Physical Intelligence

How well your understand your body and know what is necessary to maintain good health indicates your level of physical intelligence. Good physical health plays an important role in building a successful business, as it reduces the risks of you being unable to work due to illness and can increase your stamina. To begin improving your physical intelligence, notice how your body feels and do what is necessary to improve your health. Eating nutritious foods, taking appropriate exercise and getting enough sleep can boost energy and improve your ability to work effectively. You might also look better and feel more confident, which could improve both your personal and business relationships.

Ethical Intelligence

The level of honesty and integrity that an individual demonstrates in their dealings with other people and their ability to recognise such characteristics within themselves and others is a measure of their ethical intelligence. Although you need to do what you can to protect yourself from the minority of ruthless, selfish or corrupt people in the world, it is important to remember that most human beings are decent and willing to help others. Take responsibility for what you do, establish a good reputation, do business with people that you trust and build relationships that are based upon mutual respect.

Work Life Balance

The importance of work life balance to personal and family health and well being is widely accepted, but for many of us difficult to maintain. Running a business can make this even more of a challenge, with competing demands for your time and energy. It is though perhaps of even greater importance for the self-employed to find a good work life balance, so that they can remain healthy, both physically and mentally. If you are running your own business and become ill, then without benefits such as sick leave or co-workers who can take on your workload, your business could be at risk. Self-employment might though offer you the opportunity to find a better work life balance than when working for someone else. You might for example be able to fit your work around family commitments and avoid lengthy commutes, though good time management and self-discipline will be essential.

You could be doing a job that you do not enjoy, in order to pay the bills, but the prospect of self-employment might appear unrealistic and risky. Those with family responsibilities will probably have to plan their route to self-employment more carefully than someone who only has to consider their own financial security. For some people redundancy and lack of employment opportunities might force them to look towards self-employment. By contrast other people might dislike their job, but tolerate it because it enables them to afford an expensive lifestyle or they are looking forward to having greater freedom to do what they want after they retire. However, those spending the best years of their life doing a job they dislike, possibly for money they do not need, might find greater happiness by earning a living doing work that they find more fulfilling.

As human beings our sense of self and our place in the world shapes how we think and feel. The relationships we have with family and friends, the identity provided by our occupation and how we spend our free time all play a part. During previous generations people might have worked at the same job their entire life and felt a strong sense of identification and loyalty towards the values of fellow workers, employers and the wider community. However, with increasing job insecurity and career changing now the norm, you might find a greater level of continuity and control in your life by running your own business. This could lead to a better work life balance and an improved quality of life for yourself and your family.

Self-belief

If you have completed your market research, written a solid business plan and developed a product or service that you are confident will bring success, then believe in yourself and what you are doing. Be prepared to ask for help when you need it and learn from the advice of those with more experience, but whilst appreciating their assistance, do not assume that they know more about your business than you. For example you could be told that you have a good idea, but lack the experience or ability of those you are competing against. However, you should not allow doubts expressed by those who underestimate you to cause you to change or abandon your plans, unless you decide there is a good reason to do so. It is you who must find the energy and motivation to put in the hard work required to make your business a success.

Focus on how you can deliver value to your customers with a premium product or service that they will want to buy.

Self-doubt and fear of failure is normal, but if you enjoy and believe in what you are doing, then do not allow a current lack of qualifications, training or experience to cause you to give up. Although natural talent, superior education and knowing the right people are an advantage in life, self-belief and hard work can also lead to success. Learn any additional skills that you need, through self-education if necessary. Practice your art or craft and find customers who will appreciate the work that you create. If you fail, understand what went wrong, learn from your mistakes and be prepared to try again. Some people might make themselves feel better by putting you down or undermining your work, but do not allow the unfair judgement of those who revel in the failure of others stop you seeking new opportunities. Find inner strength and develop personal resources that will enable you to succeed. Many people who eventually find success have had to recover from failures and overcome setbacks along the way.

Fulfilling Work

Most people spend a considerable amount of time working and in addition to paying the bills our jobs are central to the sense of identity that we feel. However, many of us have at some point done jobs that we did not enjoy, either because we needed the money or in order to gain experience, with the hope that it would lead to something better. Redundancy and lack of suitable employment opportunities can also result in us taking jobs so that we can pay the bills, until we are able to find other work that we prefer. However, if people begin to lose hope that their situation will improve, a job which does not provide a sense of fulfilment can lead to feelings of depression and a loss of meaning and purpose in their life. This could happen even to individuals in well paid jobs which they find boring, perhaps due to a monotonous routine or because it does not enable them to use their skills, gain the experience they want or realise their potential.

Some people push themselves to do work which brings financial security and the respect of other people, but might still leave them feeling unfulfilled. They could begin to lose interest in the people and events around them, which might damage relationships with other people and how they engage with the world. This could result in a loss of motivation when it comes to maintaining a healthy lifestyle, leading to poor diet, lack of exercise, impaired decision making and possibly even reduced life expectancy. A high pressure job and being over worked, particularly when an individual does not feel in control of their life, can lead to increasing levels of stress and eventually burnout. This could be an even greater risk in the modern world, as technology means that we can be reached anywhere at any time and many people continue working even when they should be relaxing at home with family and friends or away on holiday.

Many people express a desire to find a way of earning a living which is fulfilling and leads to a good work life balance, challenging though that can be. Being responsible for paying bills and providing a secure family home can make it difficult to give up an existing career, risking loss of income and status. Those considering such a change, could be put off doing so and might later regret deciding to not follow their dream. However, some people decide that they would rather be doing work they enjoy, even if it requires changes in their lifestyle to make it happen. Although it can be daunting, taking steps towards starting a new career or running your own business can bring a feeling of greater control over your life, along with increased happiness, health and a sense of renewed purpose.

Happiness

Life and work can often be challenging and you could face many setbacks. When feeling unhappy and unmotivated, you could be told to maintain a positive outlook by thinking happy thoughts and recalling positive memories. However, positive thinking on its own might not be enough. Forcing yourself to smile or laugh, even if you feel sad, could help to make you feel happier, due to the release of chemicals in your body that improve your mood. By contrast putting on a grim expression might increase feelings of aggression. This indicates a relationship between our mind and body and that our actions influence how we feel about and respond to a situation. Places, things and other people can also influence our mood and when they have positive associations might cause us to feel better about ourselves, improve our outlook and make us more motivated to achieve success.

You could begin applying these principles in your own life and work, by for example smiling to make yourself feel happier or watching a funny film. If you experience feelings of insecurity, perhaps before an important meeting, assuming a powerful pose might help to boost your confidence. When putting off starting a piece of work, carrying out the first few physical steps involved could provide you with the motivation to continue through to completion. If you are struggling with your creativity then surround yourself with creative works, write down or sketch some ideas and ask yourself yes and no questions related to what you are trying to do. By behaving as though you are the person you aspire to be, living the life and doing the work you want to do, then to some extent you could begin to become that person. However, you will of course still have to put in the hard work required to develop the skills and gain the experience needed to make it a reality.

CHAPTER 4 PATHS TO SUCCESS

Finding Your Path

All human beings are unique, including you. So in the vast time and space of the Universe you should feel special, because you are. The personal challenge that confronts us all, is to find a path through life which enables us to achieve our potential and find fulfilment and success in how we live and work. This means engaging effectively with the world and the people around us and finding clarity, meaning and purpose in what we do. You might have to overcome obstacles along the way, but knowing what you want to do and why will make it more likely that you will find success. For example if you are not happy in your current job or career, you might be asking yourself why and what else you could do.

Formative Years

During our early years we are all naturally creative and keen to learn. We possess imagination and curiosity, but lack the knowledge and skills required to produce great work. Within us we have an awareness of what has been called variously an instinct, inner voice, calling or vocation, which leads us to prefer some activities more than others. For example we might enjoy solving puzzles, painting pictures, making things, mathematics, music, theatre or sport. Our interests might naturally translate into a course of study or training that could in adulthood lead to a suitable job, career path or form of self-employment.

Many of us go through school forced to study subjects we have little interest in or aptitude for, whilst being discouraged from focusing on subjects or activities that we prefer. This can be done for the noble principle of providing a well rounded education or because parents, teachers or peers push us towards studying subjects which prepare us for a particular job or career. Over time we can begin to lose interest in our studies, our inner voice falls silent and our natural creativity seems to disappear. However, some people continue to be guided by a deep sense of what they want to do with their life and it determines their course of study or training, even if this means withstanding criticism for the choices that they make.

Finding Your Way

It can be difficult reconnecting to your inner voice and sense of self. You could begin by looking at any hobbies or interests that you have, as you are likely to choose free time activities that you enjoy and which reflect your natural inclinations. Also ask yourself which subjects at school you preferred and performed best at. Your challenge is to find a way of matching your interests and aptitude to a job or career path that you can make into your life work. Try to imagine how you would feel in the future having developed superior skills in your chosen field and achieving success. Try to recall a time when you learned something so well that it began to feel effortless and intuitive. Let this feeling inspire you to begin the years of deep learning and practice required to achieve a great level of skill.

Knowing that you are on the right path will give you the energy and strength needed to overcome the many obstacles that might be in your path. If you are no longer young and need to continue earning a living as you forge a new career or start your own business, then rather than beginning from scratch you could look for ways in which to build upon your existing skills and experience. You could take your work in a new direction, towards what you want to do, along a path that will bring you greater fulfilment.

If the career path that you want to follow would involve learning new skills, you might think that you are too old to begin, but there are many examples of people finding success late in life. You might have already learned some of the skills needed to follow your chosen path, either at work or in your spare time. For example you might want to make one of your hobbies such as painting, pottery or photography into a career or business. This will require you to devote far more of your time and energy into focused study and practice of your chosen art or craft.

You could decide to attend a course, complete an apprenticeship, or undertake a period of formal education or training in your chosen discipline. You might feel self-doubt or receive criticism from others, telling you that you are not talented enough and should stick to a safe job, even though such life long security is for many people a thing of the past. However, the real risk is not following your inner voice, which is calling you to achieve excellence in what you want to do with your life, by developing your potential into a unique irreplaceable talent. When you know what you want to do and are ready to begin on your path, you need to find a way to learn the skills and gain the experience that will lead you to success in your chosen field.

Learning Skills

People sometimes give the impression that their talent is natural and inborn, but in reality it is the result of many hours of focused practice and immersing themselves in what they do. This potential exists within us all and not just an unusually gifted few. Having found your ideal path you must now devote sufficient deeply focused quality time to developing your skills. You must learn the details of your chosen art or craft, including any rules or principles, and understand the tools and materials used.

After ten thousand hours deeply learning and practicing a particular skill something seems to happen within the human brain, as it makes connections between your skills and the rest of your knowledge and sense of self. As you listen to and reconnect with your own inner voice, your trade, art or craft becomes a part of who you are and how you express yourself. The intuitive feel for what you are doing becomes hard wired into your brain, nervous system and muscle memory.

If you want to achieve superior skill in something, then you are setting out on a long journey, not rushing to a destination. Practice the details of your work and learn from your failures as well as your successes. Everyone who has achieved greatness has had to learn from their mistakes along the way and knowing you are on the right path will give you the patience and strength needed to carry on, overcoming setbacks and self-doubt.

It is essential that you go through this process feeling fully engaged with what you are doing, making connections through every fibre of your being to your inner self. You will learn more quickly and deeply than someone who isn't really into what they are doing and whilst they will become easily discouraged or distracted you will not. As you see improvements in your level of skill the more you practice, this will spur you on to get even better, in a circle of increasing returns. Your growing sense of achievement will make you want to practice even more until your work becomes a natural intuitive part of you.

Reaching a high level of skill and expertise in your chosen career, trade, art or craft will require you to devote a huge amount of quality focused time and effort to learning and practicing. Life is short and most of us also need to earn a living. Therefore whilst you must go through this process, your progress will be helped if you can find someone to work alongside who has already achieved the high level of skill that you aspire to. If you were able to work with them as their assistant or apprentice for example, you would have the opportunity to observe their style and technique, remaining open to absorbing their expertise, which could otherwise take far longer to achieve on your own.

Following years spent learning the rules, principles and traditions of your art or craft, you might find your natural creativity stifled. However, if you can combine your original imaginative mind with your rational mind and highly developed skills then you are in a position to create work of superior quality and uniqueness. This is the secret behind many of the greatest talents in fields as diverse as music, literature, the visual and performing arts, sports, science, technology, the professions, practical trades and crafts. If necessary reawaken your inner creativity, by allowing yourself to reconnect with the reality of the world and people around you, and letting it inspire your work.

Remember that you are forging your own path through life and developing your own unique talent. This process of learning from others, though it might last for five or ten years must eventually come to an end, even if that means overcoming resistance from others or doubt in your own abilities. Ultimately therefore your objective is to move on beyond those who you are learning from, so as to create your own unique work or business ideas. If you are unable to find someone to work alongside and learn from in such a way, then you could study the life and works of people in the same field as you whose work inspires you. They might be contemporary figures or people from the past, such as the designer William Morris, the artist Barbara Hepworth, the sculptor Henry Moore or the furniture designer Gustav Stickley.

The Internet can be an excellent source of information, as can libraries, but if possible try to see examples of your role models work in the real world and perhaps surround yourself with pictures of them and their work to assist the process of immersing yourself in their world during this time. Whilst you might initially imitate the work of others, you must eventually develop your own unique style drawing upon your inner voice and creativity. When you feel ready to do so, be guided by your inner voice to establish yourself independently and go out on your own in your chosen line of work, finding the energy to do so from your inner drive and confidence that you are on the right path.

Human Society

Many people doubt that the development of great skill and talent is within the reach of all human beings. They have been taught to believe that such abilities are the preserve of an unusually gifted few, who were born with innate natural talent or even genius. If people are unaware of the processes involved in acquiring such talents, this can provide a reassuring excuse for not trying to develop their own skills. However, there is a very sound basis for stating that we can all develop exceptional talent, provided we choose something in which we have a genuine interest and if we are prepared to devote the time and energy required to achieve it. We can begin to understand this when we look at the evolution of our species, the roots of our talents and abilities and how we have been shaped as individuals by society.

For many thousands of years our ancestors lived as hunter gathers and in our natural state we were vulnerable to many dangers. However, millions of years of evolution have equipped we humans with brains and bodies which enabled us to achieve an intuitive understanding of our natural environment and learn the skills required to build the tools that we needed to survive. Growing up in socially interdependent communities we learned complex skills, which after years of practice became so deeply ingrained within experienced individuals that what they had learned became an intuitive part of them. No longer having to recall each step in a process or task, once hardwired into their brain and nervous system, they could perform actions easily and quickly, whilst their conscious minds remained alert to their surroundings and any threats or opportunities.

The ability of our great ape relatives to demonstrate a sense of their own individuality, empathy with others and to learn skills, proves that such capacities are deep within us all at a preverbal level. However, complex spoken language enabled people to share more complex information and stories, creating organised cultures, which passed this knowledge from generation to generation. Together we learned to understand and predict predator and prey animal behaviour, the cycles of the seasons, navigate by sun moon and stars, remember where to find and how to cook food and how to construct shelters to protect us from the elements. Some people found that they had a greater interest in particular activities and so they devoted more time and energy to developing relevant knowledge and skills. This could bring them respect and praise from other members of their community and a greater sense of personal fulfilment. Such individuals were more likely to become influential and successfully pass on these characteristics to future generations.

The development of agriculture led to more settled societies, which grew in size to become the first towns, cities and nations. Recorded history began with the development of the written word, which enabled far more knowledge to be accumulated and passed on to future generations. These civilisations required increasingly advanced skills in the arts and crafts, along with the many other practical, academic, social and political skills necessary to live and work in such complex societies. It was not possible for each person to learn everything and this led to the development of many trade and professional occupations, some of which continue in their modern forms to the present day.

During previous centuries people were born into a particular social class, which often limited their life options. Most were peasants forced to work the land, whilst others followed their parents into a trade or craft, regardless of personal preference. Few beyond the wealthy elite had the opportunity to learn to read and write, with freedom and time to pursue a subject of study purely because it was of interest to them. Life is also short, competitive and requires us to learn many practical and social skills. Whilst there are still many inequalities in the world, increasingly people are being born into societies where education is widely available and most people are no longer restricted in their choice of occupation by coincidence of birth.

Our minds and bodies still possess the potential to achieve the level of deeply intuitive understanding of the natural world and skills which were essential for the survival of our early ancestors. This ability is what allows some individuals, who find that they are drawn by interest or inclination to certain activities such as an art or craft, to become especially proficient after years of practice. It is true that some people benefit from being born into wealth, having good connections or random good luck. However, each of us can decide to develop knowledge and skills that will increase our chances of achieving success, provided we remain on the path that our inner voice guides us along and make some good decisions along the way.

The Creative Process

Being able to come up with new ideas and create original work are valuable skills, that could lead to greater success in your chosen field. Although most of us would like to be more creative in our work, many consider creativity to be the preserve of a gifted few. Once thought of as almost mystical, there are now more rational explanations for the creative process. We receive a huge variety of information though our senses, some of which we are consciously aware of, but much of which we are not. The human brain processes information which can be stored as memories and used to form ideas by making connections between different pieces of information. It is therefore possible to develop a practical approach to creativity and many successful people have described stages in their creative process, which you could apply to your own work.

It can be helpful to think of the creative process as having seven stages, which could be described as objective, research, distraction, ideas, evaluation, decision and action. Your first step is to decide upon an objective, which might for example be to design an original product or develop a new business strategy. Try to break the problem down into constituent parts, so that it is easier to understand. The research stage could involve extensive reading and studying of relevant information, immersing yourself in work created by other people that entertains and inspires you or carrying out surveys among a relevant sample audience. You should then take a step back and do other things, allowing time for your subconscious mind to work on the objective using information that you have provided. During this time stop consciously thinking about what you are working on and find distraction by doing other things, such as watching a movie, playing sports and games or socialising.

Within your subconscious mind, connections, patterns and relationships between information can begin to take shape and ideas can begin to form. Many of these will be irrelevant or unsuitable, however when your mind finds some combination that matches your objective, the idea could float up to your conscious mind. Once aware of these ideas, you should make a note of them, so that they are not forgotten. Do not worry at this stage about finding complete solutions, but rather enjoy receiving the results from your earlier efforts. After you have collected enough ideas, begin to evaluate each of them, looking for potential solutions. During this stage you could also seek the opinions of other people. Eventually you will need to make a decision as to which idea you are going to implement and then take the action required to do so. The various stages of the creative process might need to be repeated a number of times, until you find a solution to your objective that you are satisfied with.

When you are working on a project consisting of a number of different objectives, they might each be at a different stage of the creative process. If you experience a creative block or circumstances cause a delay, you could work on a different objective or take a break to replenish your reserves of creative energy. Although new ideas might seem to appear from nowhere in a flash of inspiration, they are likely the result of many hours or days of work and immersion in relevant subject matter. If you are employed by someone who does not understand the creative process, they could demand instant solutions or accuse you of not working hard enough, particularly during the distraction or idea stage. Whilst having a reasonable time scale to complete a piece of work can focus attention, particularly during the research, evaluation and action stages, trying to consciously force the creative process could lead to frustration and failure. Creative inspiration does not happen on command or according to a timetable. However, you should guard against procrastination or lack of focus when needed.

Achieving Your Potential

Listen to your inner voice, which can be both supportive and constructively critical of your work, but do not become overly self-critical. Learn to graciously accept genuine praise for your work. If you are a perfectionist, learn to accept when a piece of work is finished, so that you can move on to something new. Be kind to yourself, as pushing too hard for too long could be counter productive, by making you increasingly unhappy and stressed, leading to poor mental and physical health. However, it can help with personal motivation to set yourself realistic targets and deadlines to aim for. You could give yourself a treat if you achieve your objectives and set new targets if you miss them. For example when preparing for an upcoming art exhibition or craft fair, you might aim to make a certain number of items by a particular date.

Realising your potential can help you to find purpose and direction. It can also bring with it a sense of perspective, feelings of fulfilment and a deeper connection to reality. Although many things that happen in life might be beyond your control, you can decide how you feel about and respond to events. Make the most of challenging situations, recognising opportunities and staying on track to follow your own path. Many people have experienced setbacks in their life, but whilst some might have given up others persevered, often learning more from their failures than their successes. Allow for random events and outside influences, which could inspire your work. Even when we are busy doing other things or sleeping our subconscious continues to make connections between the different pieces of information in our mind, which could lead to new ideas and solutions to problems.

Following years of involvement in a particular subject, those with a receptive engaged mind could begin forming deeper connections in their brain, leading to patterns of information that inspire new creative insights. For example an artist might develop a new style through which to express themselves, or a craft maker could develop a new technique, enabling them to make work of superior quality. Many years of patient study, practice and hard work can bear fruit as your skills and talents become an intuitive part of who you are. You can enjoy the details of the process of your work, rather than just the end goal. This will give you the energy you need to push through creative blocks and setbacks. You will even learn from your mistakes, as they show you how not to do things and take you closer to finding the solutions that you seek.

Develop and maintain an holistic outlook in your life and work, allowing ideas to form, take shape and connect in your mind. The social, emotional, intellectual, creative and rational parts of your brain are all interconnected and together with your memories, experiences, knowledge and skills form who you are. Be self-aware, even to a primal elemental level, remaining connected to who you are and what you do and stay actively engaged with and interested in the people around you and the world in which you live. When you get mental and creative blocks, don't let them discourage you and instead look for ways to work through or around them. If you get bored with your work, then you could try a new style or approach. Finding your way back to fresh original creativity could sometimes mean beginning again on a piece of work, which might lead to improvements when you look at it from a new perspective and with renewed energy.

Personal Development

Human beings are naturally creative and as an artist or craft maker you have the opportunity to express your individual creativity. Knowing that you want to do something is the first step towards making it a reality, as this will enable you to focus your energies on doing what is needed to achieve your goals. Try to understand the motivations of other people, how your behaviour affects them, how they want to be perceived and what path they are following. The choices that you make and how you relate to the people and the world around you will influence your path and inform the work that you create. Remember to enjoy the journey, learn from your mistakes and believe in yourself, rather than dwelling too much upon the past or worrying unduly about the future.

In what can be a lonely and confusing world, many of us want to find meaning and purpose in our life and work. Therefore the path to success that you follow should be of your own choosing rather than being planned only to please other people. Although having goals and ambitions can motivate us to achieve more than we might otherwise have thought we were capable, try not to place too much pressure upon yourself. Whether looking for your first job or leaving behind a career that you have done for many years to start a new business, you should decide what you want to do with your life. If your ambition is to earn a living from doing work that brings you a sense of personal fulfilment, you could look for inspiration from those who have done so before you and find support from others on a similar path. You might also find fulfilment through helping other people, for example by teaching a course or workshop and motivating others by sharing with them some of your skills and experience.

Modern life and work can mean that we are constantly interacting either in person or online, leaving us feeling overwhelmed by the pressure to keep up. This can lead to stress, loss of sleep and poor decision making, damaging our physical and mental well being. You should therefore include some time each day during which distractions such as electronic devices are switched off, so that you are able to properly relax and rebuild your physical and mental energy levels. For some people this could involve taking a walk through a park or along the beach, whilst others might prefer to meditate or take a relaxing bath. This time spent alone with your own thoughts could allow you to connect with your inner sense of self. If you experience a creative block or are struggling with a difficult problem, you could ask yourself some relevant questions and allow answers to form in your mind. This might provide a fresh perspective and lead to new ideas and solutions.

The Art of Doing Nothing

Some people feel they are being lazy if they are not always busy doing something. However, when done properly, you should consider time each day spent doing nothing to be an investment in your well being. It can reduce stress, improve health and increase productive creativity when you are ready to work. The art of doing nothing has long been practised by students of meditation. To begin doing nothing yourself, find a place free from distractions, such as a quiet room in your home. Make yourself comfortable and relax, perhaps by gently tensing and then relaxing the muscles from your feet and legs, up your body to your head. Close your eyes, clear your mind of thoughts, calm your mind and breathe slowly and deeply in and out. Initially this could be done for a few minutes each day and over a period of weeks gradually increased, to perhaps half an hour or more.

When you feel ready to do so, start practicing these techniques outside, perhaps in a garden or park. Focus on the sounds and smells around you, before opening your eyes to appreciate the beauty of the natural world. Eventually you could begin practicing the art of doing nothing whilst carrying out daily activities. For example whilst eating and drinking, so that you enjoy the taste of each mouthful which is slowly consumed, rather than being rushed down. Practice when you are in a busy public space, taking a break at work, using public transport or standing in a queue. Rather than using your mobile phone or reading a newspaper, be in the moment, observing the people and the events taking place around you. Relax and focus upon the information that you are receiving through your five senses. You will probably become aware of things, which other people are too busy to notice.

Time and Money

Few people are wealthy enough that they do not need to work in order to pay for essentials, such as food and shelter. Most of us also like to be able to purchase luxuries for ourselves or those close to us and many people want to support charities or causes that are important to them. Beyond a certain point though, the amount of money that a person has at their disposal might not bring them as much happiness as having enough time. However, people will often plan their career around the amount of money that they can earn and work longer hours to buy things they could live without. If you follow the path towards self-employment, then you might be able to structure your working day to suit the needs of your life and your business, rather than the dictates of an employer. Although you might find yourself under greater financial pressure and need to work far harder than when employed by others, working for yourself can give you a feeling of self-empowerment.

Rather than the things we buy, our memories are dominated by the relationships that we have with other people and our experiences either alone or with others. Unlike money, we cannot increase the amount of time that we have, therefore you should think carefully about how you spend your time. People are generally happier sharing their time with family and friends, rather than those they meet when working. We also value having the freedom to decide what we are going to do and when and prefer to be involved in activities that we enjoy, such as a favourite hobby. If your work provides you with a healthy level of stimulation and the feeling that you are doing something worthwhile with your life, then you are more likely to be happy and feel a sense of fulfilment.

Beyond the essentials, when spending money ask yourself whether it will improve the quality of your life or the lives of other people. For example you could hire an experienced professional to carry out a particular task, which you either lack the necessary skill or time to do yourself. They will probably be able to complete the work more quickly and to a higher standard than you would be able to achieve. Spending money in this way could allow you to focus your energies on other activities and devote more time to family and friends. You would also be providing the opportunity for someone else to earn a living. You could pay for experiences, such as travelling to a place that you would like to visit, attending cultural events, buying labour saving devices, or purchasing items that could inspire you, such as a work of art or handmade craft.

Resistance To Change

As an entrepreneur setting up your own business, you are trying to make a change in your life and the world around you. However, individuals and organisations are often resistant to change and prefer to follow the familiar path that promises a safe outcome. Consequently when forging a new path you should be prepared to receive criticism and experience rejection from other people. Rather than getting upset or angry at the negative opinions of others, accept that this is normal, as you are breaking new ground, which could lead to success or failure. Remain positive and put your energy into what you need to do to succeed, instead of being distracted by those who would prefer you to give up or predict you will fail. Uncertainty regarding how they might be affected by change can make people feel uncomfortable. Also if you are successful this could force others to question the choices they have made and confront them with difficult decisions about their own life.

Although you might meet resistance to change from other people, you should also be aware of it within yourself. Listen to the constructive criticism of others and be prepared to make changes to your business if they become necessary. There are many examples of once successful creative individuals or companies becoming set in their ways and failing to recognise or make the most of new opportunities. Do not assume that current success will continue for ever. Learn from your mistakes and be open to new ideas and better ways of doing things. Remain adaptable to changes in fashion, taste and technology and responsive to new competition. The world is an ever changing place and if it becomes clear that what you are currently doing will not lead you to the success you seek, then you should be prepared to find a new path to success.

Decision Making

When you are running a business you will need to have the confidence to make often difficult decisions. However, we can find ourselves under pressure to make important decisions before we are ready and this can sometimes lead to mistakes that we later regret. This could be because a delay is not possible, however sometimes we are being pressured by other people who have priorities which might not be in our best interests. For example a salesperson could be trying to close a sale in order to increase their commission. Rather than allowing yourself to be forced into making decisions before you are ready to do so, you should focus on the benefits you are looking for. Take the time you need to consider the relevant information and potential consequences. Also avoid making decisions too rashly when you are feeling overwhelmed, under too much stress and not thinking clearly. Without wasting time, try if possible to delay decision making until you have evaluated a situation and can make a decision that is right for yourself and your business.

Celebrate Success

When setting up a new business, an inspiring mission statement and motivational vision statements can give you goals to aim for and a path to follow. Also you can benefit from a sense of fulfilment when doing work that you enjoy. However, building a business can be a difficult and lonely experience. You should therefore celebrate success, such as reaching a target or milestone, attracting a new client for your work or receiving a lucrative commission. A successful business is built upon the talent and hard work of its founders, delivering what their customers want. However, there is often a wider support network of people helping them, such as family, friends, mentors, colleagues or employees. Including these people in your celebrations could be a way for you to show them that you appreciate what they have done to help you. A small celebration, such as a meal at a local restaurant, could also provide some happy memories, that might help to boost your energy levels and self-belief when you are going through tough times.

CHAPTER 5 YOUR CUSTOMERS

Attracting Customers

If you want to run a successful business, then you must attract a sufficient number of customers for the products or services that you are selling. Consumers have access to a wide range of information and choice when it comes to their buying decisions and the better you understand and fulfil their wants and needs the more likely they are to buy from you. Before making a purchase, people will often spend time online and in real life researching products and services, reading reviews and comparing what is available. Building your business upon something that you have a passion for, such as an art or craft, has advantages compared to a business driven solely by financial considerations. You are more likely to take a pride in your work and feel motivated to devote the time and effort needed to provide products and services that are of superior quality. This could be reflected in your branding and marketing, attracting customers who will appreciate what you are selling.

Your Audience

When deciding who the audience will be for what you are planning to sell, avoid the temptation of trying to appeal to everyone by being a jack of all trades. Instead you are more likely to find success if you can establish your reputation within a lucrative niche. One of the challenges of building a successful business is looking for ways to either reduce costs or increase prices, so that the overall business revenue is sufficient to cover running costs and leave a profit. Therefore rather than trying to compete purely on price, focus on quality and look for ways that you can provide your customers with added value. A business selling a mass market commodity will often compete on price, resulting in a small per unit profit margin and rely on a high volume of sales to generate sufficient revenue. However, an arts and crafts business making handmade work will be selling fewer items by comparison and will therefore need to generate a greater level of profit from each sale.

When planning your marketing strategy think carefully about the customers that you want to reach and how you will engage with them. You could play to your strengths as a small business, by emphasising how much you value each and every customer, which can be in stark contrast to the experiences people often have when dealing with large organisations. Highlight the quality of what you are selling, so that you differentiate yourself from less expensive competitors. If you spend your marketing budget attracting customers who are concerned more about cost than quality, this could result in a lower profit margin from each sale and less money to invest in growth. Customers shopping around for bargains might also be less likely to make multiple purchases from your business, potentially wasting the time and money that you invested in attracting them. Having existing customers who are keen to purchase more from you, can reduce your marketing costs and you could use some of the money saved to reward customer loyalty, by for example including an unexpected free gift with some of their purchases.

Customer Surveys

Having decided upon the product or service that you are going to sell, you will need to identify your target audience and know how to engage with them effectively, so as to turn them into customers. You could begin this process by using surveys to gather relevant information about potential customers, such as their interests and demographic data. Many organisations use online services which enable them to collect and analyse customer survey data to assist their decision making. When people visit your website you could ask them questions such as how they found the site, what they are looking for and whether the site helped them. You could also ask people for their name and email address and request their agreement to receiving more information in the future. If you are going to be attending an event, perhaps selling your work at a craft fair or holding an art exhibition, you could take with you some printed copies of the survey forms. To encourage people to complete and return the paper forms, they could be entered into a prize draw with the chance to win something appropriate, such as an art set or a craft kit.

When creating your customer surveys, the questions that you ask could relate to the type of products or services that you sell. For example you could ask if they have purchased something similar in the past, where and how they found it, what influenced their buying decisions and whether there were particular features that they either liked or disliked. You could ask what might have put them off buying such things in the past, whether there is something they would like to buy if it was available and what they would consider to be a reasonable price to pay. Answers to such questions could indicate what people want to buy and why, highlighting opportunities and helping you to plan ahead. However, try not to overwhelm people with too many questions, as this might put them off completing the survey. You would need a sample size that is large enough to provide the necessary insights into customer behaviour. The information that you collect from your surveys could be used to create profiles and plan marketing strategies designed to attract your target audience and convert them into customers.

Customer Communications

In all of your communications with potential or existing customers, as well as colleagues, suppliers and the media, you are representing yourself and your business. Listen to your customers, understand their perspective and treat them in a way that demonstrates your respect for them. It is human nature to prefer spending time with people that we like and trust and this also applies to the businesses we chose to buy products or services from. Engage with your customers using an appropriate tone and style of communication and be ready to answer their questions. When providing a service such as teaching an art or craft or working on a commission, you might sometimes need to politely explain to a client that in your opinion they are wrong. Remember that they are paying for your expertise, so do not be afraid to remind them that they can rely upon your skill and experience. It is important that you gain the trust of your customers in all of your interactions with them. Without being arrogant, express confidence in what you do, as you cannot expect customers to trust in your abilities if you do not.

The perception that people have of your business will become the reality to them and influence the way that they describe you to other people. Therefore having established a brand identity, mission statement and core values for your business, try to always reflect them. You could meet a potential customer unexpectedly in a social or business setting, so be ready with a short sentence describing what you do. If you have an inspiring story or funny anecdote relating to how you started your business, telling this to someone that you meet could help them to remember you. First impressions matter and you might have only one opportunity to attract a new customer. Do not risk losing existing customers by allowing the quality of your communications to decline. Always acknowledge assistance that you receive, thanking those involved and where possible returning favours. Remain honest and genuine in all of your dealings, as having a good reputation is an important part of building a successful business.

Premium Products and Services

When you are selling a premium product or service, you will need customers who appreciate a superior level of quality, attention to detail and excellent customer care. For example as an artist or craft maker you could use the best materials and tools, which combined with your expert skills, will enable you to create items that meet or exceed your customers exacting standards. In order for a business to be able to afford the investment of time and money required to develop premium products or services, it will have to attract customers who are willing and able to pay for them. Reaching an audience through suitably targeted marketing, could mean investing more in the cost of customer acquisition (COCA). Although providing premium products and services will probably increase your costs, you could benefit from the higher lifetime value (LTV) of each customer and an increased profit margin. People buying from you might also write positive reviews or testimonials and recommend your work to their family and friends, helping your business to grow.

If you want to establish a premium brand, then you will need to consider every stage at which your customers could engage with your business. This will include the design of all marketing materials, your website, stationery and how you dress if you meet them. First impressions will be formed by how well your products are boxed or wrapped and the content of any communications should reflect the qualities of your brand. For example if you decide to put together art or craft kits, ensure that in addition to including any necessary materials or tools, they are sold with quality packaging and suitable instructions.

Pay attention to details such as using correct customer names and personalising the buying experience by including a handwritten thank you note with each sale. Ensure excellent service from first contact, through to purchase, delivery, after sales support and ongoing engagement. Maintain a professional level of presentation at any events that you organise or attend. For example if you are selling work at a craft fair, you should set up a well designed table display. Although you might be more expensive than your competitors, such efforts on your part will enhance the perceived value of your products and services and remind customers why they chose you.

Email Marketing

The rise of social media has caused some people to claim that it could replace email as a way of reaching customers. However, a good email marketing strategy can help you to develop channels of communication with potential customers and engage more effectively with existing customers. Many of us check our mailbox frequently during the course of a typical day. However, most of the emails that we receive will probably end up being deleted, either unread or without their content being acted upon. Therefore the challenge is to craft emails which attract the attention of your target audience, by having appropriate subject lines and content which is relevant, personalised and includes direct calls to action with clear customer benefits.

Before trying to sell your products or services to a customer, you will probably have greater success if you first build a relationship with them, by demonstrating the interests and concerns that you both share. Try to keep email messages that you send short and with a specific purpose in mind. You can cover other points in additional emails, though you should remember to include an unsubscribe option, so that you are sending emails to people who are receptive to them. When planning your email marketing strategy, there are several basic elements. You will need to provide a means by which people can opt in to begin receiving emails and a place where you can store each name and email address, along with any relevant demographic data. In addition to having an application in which you can compose emails, you will also need to manage the sending of emails and the tracking of data such as open rates and click through rates.

If you posses the necessary technical skills, you could develop a system to manage the email process, but you will probably decide to use an email marketing service. Such services will generally provide forms that subscribers can complete, along with a database in which to store data, templates to help you design attractive emails and software to manage and analyse your email campaigns. When deciding which email marketing service to use, read reviews and compare the features each offers, so that you can find a service which is within your budget and suits your requirements. Regarding frequency of email messages to new customers, you could initially send one each day, then one every few days and eventually one a week or one a month. Monitor the effectiveness of the emails that you send, which should be designed to provide information to those receiving them that is both relevant and timely.

In addition to sending regular emails to existing customers, in which you could write about topical issues of interest to them, create a series of autoresponder emails, designed to engage with potential customers at each stage of their journey. The purpose of autoresponder emails is to motivate people to continue along a path that will build a long term relationship and might eventually lead to them purchasing a particular product or service from your business. The content of each email will depend upon your objective, for example you could begin by introducing your product or service and demonstrating how it could benefit the potential customer. Within subsequent emails, you could include narratives highlighting your skills and experience, provide reviews or testimonials and introduce new products or services. When creating email messages, write with an appropriate style that reflects the personality of your brand.

Across all of the autoresponder emails sent in a sequence you should maintain a consistent tone and provide evidence that instills a sense of confidence and trust in your business. The number of emails within a sequence might range from just a few to dozens and the frequency from daily to weekly, depending upon the number you feel is sufficient. Having written your emails, you could ask a friend or family member to read them in sequence and ask for their feedback. Analyse the performance of autoresponder emails over time, looking at factors such as open rate, click through rate (CTR), forward or unsubscribe rate and how effectively they convert prospects into paying customers.

From the first time a potential customer visits your website and sends an enquiry, through to their initial purchase and beyond, you should be able to manage and evaluate the process, measuring data such as open and conversion rates. Think carefully about the email subject line and content, possibly split testing them to compare the effectiveness of different emails. Incentives that could encourage people to supply their name and email address and agree to receive emails from you could include a free newsletter subscription, posting comments on your blog, access to online courses or arts and crafts guides. You could also encourage people who you meet through social media to visit your website and subscribe to your email list.

When you have established a good relationship with your customers, they will probably be happy to receive the occasional email from you, provided they find it useful and it doesn't come across as just another sales or marketing message. Use information that they have supplied, such as their preferences and past purchases, to send emails that are personalised, written in an entertaining style and relevant to their interests and needs. If you link to any custom landing pages on your website, ensure that the content complements the information in the email. You could also write some standard emails to send in response to common questions that you receive, adapting the content so as to be relevant to the specific situation they refer to.

Customer Data

As your business begins to attract more customers and the volume of communication and information increases, it can become increasingly difficult to effectively manage the data that accumulates. In the past there would have been filing cabinets full of client documents, contact details recorded in address books, meeting notes written in diaries and telephone messages written on pieces of paper. A considerable amount of effort was required to manage this information, often collected by different people over many months and years. The inability to quickly and easily gather together all of the information relating to a specific customer could lead to poor service and lost sales. By the latter part of the twentieth century, many businesses had begun to use computers with office software, such as spreadsheets, and there was a rapid growth in the use of the Internet and Email. Whilst this enabled large amounts of data to be collected and stored electronically, the retrieval and analysis of information was often inefficient and time consuming.

The need for a reliable method for managing customer data led to the development of Customer Relationship Management (CRM) software, which stores data within a relational database. CRM software can be used by a business to manage and automate tasks involved in sales, marketing and customer service. It can be used to keep a record of all forms of communication between the business and each of their potential and existing customers, including emails, social media, telephone calls, direct mail and real life meetings. This makes it easier for a business to track and analyse sales leads and conversions, provide a more personalised customer experience and increase customer retention. Examples of popular CRM software include Salesforce, which charges a fee based upon the number of users, and the open source SuiteCRM. There are many other CRMs available and the choice of which to use would depend upon your requirements and available resources.

The use of CRM software can enable a business to manage and analyse data more efficiently, enabling them to develop better long term customer relationships, rather than focusing on short term sales targets. However, when you are planning to use a CRM, it is important that you have a clear reason for collecting particular information and a strategy for how it will be used. For example you might want to be able to plan better marketing campaigns, spot seasonal sales patterns and identify your most loyal customers, so that you can reward them in some way. Collecting vast volumes of data without clearly defined reasons for doing so can lead to a business being overwhelmed or distracted, rather than focusing on the key data that can help them to improve performance and increase profits.

In addition to customer data, other common business requirements include managing orders, accounting, invoicing, controlling stock levels, storing employee records, managing supplier relationships and attending or planning events. The objectives when managing business data could include increased efficiency savings and reduced running costs and this could involve the use of Enterprise Resource Planning (ERP) software. Although customer and business data will often be managed using separate systems, benefits can sometimes be gained from the integration of data, by highlighting opportunities to reduce costs or increase revenue and profits. There is a wide range of software available for managing your customer and business data and the choice of which to use will depend upon your available budget and business requirements. Open source software can be used without paying a fee and allows the user to modify the source code to suit their needs, though this could involve bringing in outside support. Proprietary software suppliers retain rights over the source code and charge their customers a fee, though a business might decide that the software provides a solution that meets their particular requirements.

Managing Complaints

Most people understand that no matter how hard you work to provide excellent customer service, accidents and mistakes can happen. However, customers will judge your response to any complaints. When you become aware of a problem you should look into it promptly, keeping your customers updated on what you are doing to resolve the issue. For example if you cancel an event that you were going to run, then as early as possible you should inform people who were going to attend and refund any payments they have made. If you are unable to run an event due to circumstances beyond your control, but have taken out the relevant insurance cover, then this should help to minimise your losses.

You should offer to refund or replace a customer purchase, if an item that has been posted to them either does not arrive or is delivered damaged. It is better under such circumstances to accept a financial loss and maintain good customer relations, rather than risk losing future sales. You should also look into the availability of compensation cover. However, a situation could arise in which the fault is not with your business and there is nothing that you can do to fix a particular problem, in which case you should politely explain what action the customer needs to take. If you are unable to provide a solution to a customer complaint or they become unreasonable, then you could decide that it is better to offer them a refund and possibly suggest they might be happier finding another business to meet their future needs.

Recommendations Reviews and Testimonials

Asking existing clients to recommend you to their family and friends could be an effective way of attracting new customers. You could contact people by email after they make a purchase to see if they are happy with what they have bought and request that they write a review or testimonial. They might welcome the opportunity to help other people with useful advice. You could provide a section within your website featuring what they have written. Customers might decide to show off what they have bought from you by posting pictures online to share with other people. When your work is discussed on a forum, blog or social media platform, then you should respond appropriately, which could include retweeting or liking some posts. People will often respond more to what they are told in person, compared to something appearing online. You should therefore make the most of each opportunity to speak to other people, for example when attending events.

Think carefully about where you will be using reviews and testimonials and what you hope to achieve with them. General feedback about your business can be helpful, but those going into more detail about the features of a product or service can be more effective. Customers will often have particular concerns at certain stages of the engagement process and ideally a review or testimonial will answer their questions when they occur to them, without raising other issues that could complicate matters unnecessarily. Understanding the customer journey and what motivates people to continue at each stage, can help you to ask relevant questions when requesting testimonials or reviews. Try to be specific, rather than asking vague or open ended questions, whilst still allowing your customers the freedom to provide accurate and credible answers. You could ask someone who fits the customer profile to use your website and observe them as they do so. Take note of any issues they encounter and relevant questions that arise, as they go through the customer journey.

When buying a premium product or service, people look for indicators of quality and reliability. Compared to less expensive alternatives, there should be fewer reasons for customer dissatisfaction, complaints and negative comments or reviews. However, if you receive a genuine complaint, highlighting an issue that needs to be addressed, view this positively as an opportunity to improve your business. It is better that an unhappy customer contacts you, rather than you hearing nothing but losing future sales. You should therefore make it easy for customers to contact you with their questions, suggestions or complaints. When you are able to resolve a problem to the customers satisfaction, they might appreciate the level of customer support they have received and as a result post a positive review. This would indicate to other people reading such a review that you run a business providing good customer service. Compared to a piece of paid advertising, or self-promotion done by a business, people reading genuine recommendations, reviews or testimonials are more likely to trust them and be positively influenced in their buying decisions.

CHAPTER 6 YOUR BUSINESS WEBSITE

Do You Need A Website?

Having a website is widely considered to be an essential part of running a successful business. Potential clients will often search the Internet to learn more about your business and this provides an opportunity to attract customers that you might not otherwise reach. A well designed website with relevant engaging content can help to form a positive opinion of your business and instil confidence when customers are considering purchasing your products or services. It is important to make a good impression when people first visit your site and reinforce this each time they return. Your website can improve communication with customers, market and sell your work and promote your business brand. In this chapter we will provide a basic overview of some of the technology and concepts used in the production and running of a website, so that even if you are getting someone else to design and develop your site, you will have some understanding of what is involved.

Website Technology

A website consists of a number of web pages, which are documents written in hypertext markup language (HTML), that can be stored on a server and delivered over the Internet. A web browser can interpret the HTML, rendering the page and displaying content such as text and hyperlinks, used to navigate between web pages. Other content can be included within web pages, such as photographs, audio and video. After website files have been uploaded to the server that you are using to host your website and because the server is connected to the Internet, when a visitor goes to your domain name using their web browser they can see your website. Cascading Style Sheets (CSS) provide a more efficient way to instruct a browser on how to format the appearance of web pages. JavaScript is a scripting language that is interpreted by browsers and can be used to add greater functionality to web pages.

HTML, CSS and JavaScript are in common use and supported by popular Web browsers, such as Chrome, Internet Explorer, Firefox, Safari and Opera. There can however be differences in the way that each browser interprets and renders web pages. Static pages created using basic HTML will display the same web page content to each visitor. HTML5 offers the potential to provide more interactive media content, without the need for plugin software such as Flash Player or Java. However, there is often a need for websites with advanced functionality and the capacity to store and retrieve database data, such as eCommerce sites managing financial transactions and forums that require members to login. These websites can be developed using programming languages such as PHP or ASP.NET, that are processed on the server and return results which are then displayed in the browser.

Domain Names

A domain name is a convenient way of representing the numerical IP address used to identify the location on the hosting server where your website files are stored. It is also an important part of your business identity and branding. Having a name which includes important keywords can help with search engine traffic and make it clear to potential customers what products or services you sell. You can search for available domain names online and either register a name with the company you plan to host your site with or use a different company. Finding an appropriate domain name that is available to register can be difficult, though you might be able to purchase one from the current owner. However, it is worthwhile taking some time over your search, until you find a name that you will be happy with during the months and years ahead, as you promote and grow your business. You could for example combine one of your main keywords with your name or location. Take care though to not choose a domain name which conflicts with or is confusingly similar to an established website, brand or trademark.

When registering a domain name for your business website, you will have to decide which Top Level Domain (TLD) to use. Ideally this will be the international commercial extension .com, although if you are operating within a specific country then you might prefer a country level domain, for example .co.uk within the United Kingdom or .us within the United States. To protect your brand, you might decide to register other popular extensions such as .org and .net, along with variations of your domain, for example both plural and singular versions. Many less popular extensions are also available, although building your website on one of them could mean losing traffic, as people might go to a website using the same name, but with an extension they are more familiar with. Available domain names can generally be registered cheaply, but it might be expensive to buy a domain name from someone else who has already registered it, though this might be a worthwhile investment.

Planning Your Website

For some businesses a simple brochure style website might be all that is needed. However, if you are selling a wide range of products or services with many personalised features, your business will probably benefit from having something more substantial. Paying for experienced professionals to design and develop your website could be a worthwhile investment. A good website can present a professional image, reflecting the quality of products or services that you sell. If you hire a design agency, they might also be able to provide you with online marketing services, giving you more time and energy to focus on your work.

Visitors to a website will generally experience it as a number of pages that have been linked together. Websites have a home page, which appears as the first page when visitors enter the domain name into their browser. A contact page will typically have enquiry forms and contact details such as the postal address and telephone numbers. The about us page could introduce the business owner or employees and provide a brief biography of the business. Many websites will also have a page with terms and conditions and another for the privacy policy. Other pages could include those describing products or services and landing pages, designed as a destination for marketing campaigns. Some sites also make use of more advanced functionality such as blogs or eCommerce.

When planning your website you should have a clear idea of what you want it to do for your business, for example promoting a product and getting sales leads. Each of the elements in the structure and content of a site should play a part in achieving those goals. The use of Wireframes and persona journeys, focusing on how people will use a site, can be of great value during the web design process. You cannot be sure which page visitors will initially land on when they visit your site, therefore it is important that every page engages effectively with them. If what someone is looking for is on another page, it should be possible for them to find it easily.

From Planning to Deployment

The typical process for creating a new website will begin with planning, which could be done using pen and paper, before moving on to the development environment, where the software can be built and tested. After being designed and developed, the website could then be moved to a staging server, which simulates the live environment, enabling end to end testing to be carried out. This should ensure that the site is functioning as expected, before it is used by the general public. The website can then be deployed to the production server and made live, so that people can begin visiting the site. Subsequently additional design and development work on the website can be done safely, in an environment that is separate from the live site. Updates, feature changes and new functionality can then be installed on the live site after they have been properly tested.

Well designed web pages, with user friendly navigation can improve usability, enhance brand recognition, increase content stickiness and boost sales conversions. However, if you have designed your own website, then you might not be the best judge of how well it performs. Before launching a website, you should therefore ask a representative sample of people to test the site. Request feedback regarding functionality and usability. Observe how people move around the site, so that you can spot any potential navigation or usability issues and ask them how they found the experience. Look out for obstacles that could get in the way of visitors finding what they are looking for and any improvements that could be made.

When your site is up and running you could use services such as Google Analytics, which provides anonymised statistical data. For example you can see which pages people land on, pages they visit, which links they click on within each page, how long they remain on a page and where they exit the site. This could help you to measure the effectiveness of a marketing campaign and monitor how changes to the site influence the way that people use it. You could also run A/B testing, which involves splitting visitor traffic between two different versions of the same page. By observing the engagement and conversion rates resulting from each page, you could improve user experience, site performance and return on investment (ROI) at each stage of the visitor journey.

Website Visitor Engagement

When competing for audience attention, the more that you understand the people who will be visiting your website the better you will be able to meet their needs and expectations. Think about who the person landing on your website might be, how you can relate to them, what they are looking for and how you can help them to achieve their goals. Consider how each visitor might have found your site, their motivation and what each page they visit might make them think or feel. Ask yourself whether the content and user experience design moves visitors towards an objective, such as them contacting you regarding a commission or buying a piece of work. What path might they follow through your website? How well does each page match their likely mood and thought processes at that point? For example a customer could leave your website before completing a purchase, if the overall buying experience is too complex. Therefore try to limit the number of steps involved to the minimum required.

Having decided upon clear objectives that you want your website to achieve, define your intended audience, so that the site design and content is appropriate. This could include developing user profiles and splitting them into demographic and interest groups. You could map user journeys, carry out your own market research and look into consumption of other media popular with the target audience. Aim to provide a good user experience, encouraging people to become engaged with your website and your business. Make it easy for people to find content that they are looking for, which should engage effectively with them. Have a clear understanding of what you want each page to achieve and only include content that is relevant, at that point of a visitor journey, helping people to better understand something or answering potential questions. Irrelevant information can be distracting and answering the wrong questions could raise unnecessary doubts, interrupting the decision making process.

Most people prefer the path of least resistance and when confronted with too many options can become stressed, triggering the fight or flight response, causing them to leave your website too soon. When looking for an item that suits their needs, having a number of options to choose from might make it easier for people to find what they want. However, limiting someone to just two or three options can make it easier for them to make a decision. You should provide a clear easy to follow path, by providing relevant information, calls to action and hyperlinks to additional details if appropriate. When including information or testimonials, they should be relevant and answer questions that visitors might have at that stage. Helping people to make well informed decisions when it comes to their choice of a product or service is more likely to lead to satisfied customers and repeat sales.

Web Design

First impressions are important and when a visitor lands on a web page the overall visual design will influence their perception of the quality of the site and the business it represents. Good design involves the organisation of elements so that they are aesthetically pleasing, improve user experience, help to communicate information and increase engagement. Responsive web design allows the layout of web pages to respond to the device they are viewed on, adapting to large desktop screens, smaller tablet or mobile phone screens and landscape or portrait orientation. Rather than having different versions of a web page for each device type, this is achieved using techniques such as fluid grids, flexible images and CSS rules. When the design of your website is being planned, account should also be taken of whether content will change over time. Try to understand your audience and avoid overwhelming them with too much information too soon or causing confusion with poorly planned design. Unless you posses the necessary design skills, you will probably benefit from seeking the assistance of an experienced web designer.

Creating Your Website

Website markup and code could be written using a software package such as Adobe DreamWeaver or within a text editor such as Notepad. However, most complex websites are now built using a Content Management System (CMS), such as WordPress or Drupal. Decide which software to use for the development of your website and whether to do the work yourself or hire someone else. Alternatively there are a number of website builder services which provide tools that can be used to construct a website and then have it run within their shared hosting environment. Such services typically include templates to help with design and can range from basic brochure websites to eCommerce sites with back office features. However, site builder services can have limitations and might lack some of the features that you want, which could be made available when a site is developed using a CMS. Although it is important to make appropriate decisions when it comes to the technology used in the development and management of your website, they are only tools for achieving your business objectives.

Content Management Systems

During the early days of the web, it was common for websites to be hand coded, which required considerable time and skill when building complex sites. Each page of a website was a separate HTML document, linked with others using hyperlinks. Large complex websites are now generally built using a CMS (Content Management System). Content and presentation can be separated, with page text and other data stored in a database, providing an environment in which a website can be developed, published and managed efficiently. A typical CMS provides user friendly interfaces for managing elements such as text and graphics, in addition to support for multiple users, who are able to login and work on a website in a collaborative manner. For a basic website you might decide to use one of your hosting companies own template based website packages. However, compared to site builder services, a CMS can generally provide greater control and a wider range of features, that might be required in custom business solutions.

There are many different content management systems available, some open source and others proprietary. They are written in a number of programming languages and designed to run on different server software and operating systems. The most popular open source CMS software, such as WordPress, Drupal and Joomla, were written using the PHP programming language. They are typically hosted on an Apache HTTP server, running the Linux operating system and use a relational database management system (RDBMS) such as MySQL. The acronym LAMP can be used to refer to a solution stack using the four open source elements; Linux, Apache, MySQL and PHP. A solution stack is a collection of different software which when brought together produces a complete software platform. Although developers building a website with a CMS would need to posses relevant technical knowledge, non-technical people who are adding and editing content should be able to do so with relative ease.

Open Source CMS or Proprietary CMS

Open source software is not owned by anyone and popular systems such as Drupal, Joomla and WordPress have been built from coding contributions made by thousands of different developers based in countries around the world, rather than a single company. You can download an open source CMS at no charge, though some developers sell plugins with particular functionality that you might want to buy, and you will still need to pay for other costs such as the hosting of the website. A proprietary CMS developed by a company often has pre made functionality that might suit a particular business or industry sector. You will typically rent proprietary CMS software from the company that owns it, which could for example involve paying a monthly fee. When deciding whether to have your website built using an open source CMS or a proprietary CMS, the choice will depend upon your business requirements and available resources. You could begin by asking yourself some questions, such as who will be developing the website and what features will be required. To help you make a decision, you will find reviews online for both open source and proprietary software.

When you download an open source CMS, the software that you begin with will need to be configured and customised to suit your requirements. If you do not posses the necessary skills, hiring someone else to do the work for you could involve a higher upfront cost than with a proprietary CMS. However, after paying for the design and development of an open source solution, you do not need to be tied down to ongoing fees, unless you decide to pay for someone to manage your website. The many designers and developers contributing to the creation of open source software can result in their being a greater range of features than might be available from proprietary solutions. Also with an open source CMS you will have access to the original source code, enabling new features and functionality to be developed if required. You should be able to find developers with the necessary skills and experience, who are available for hire to carry out such work.

The ready to use functionality of a proprietary CMS can lessen or remove the need for you to hire someone who is able customise the CMS to meet your requirements. This could reduce the initial cost and time needed to get your website up and running. Indeed it is probable you will be unable to access the source code of a proprietary CMS and that available features will be limited to those provided by the supplier. Therefore if you choose to use a proprietary solution, you should ensure that it includes all of the features that you think your website will need. Seek reassurance from the company that they are going to provide long term support, as you will depend upon them for any future changes to the software, such as security updates. Rebuilding your website in the future using an alternative CMS could cause considerable inconvenience, costing you both time and money. You should also find out how easy or difficult it would be to export website data, for example if you ever wanted or needed to move your site to a different hosting provider.

Drupal and Wordpress

Many developers and agencies use Drupal or WordPress to deliver client websites and if you are considering using one of them, you could read reviews and ask for advice from people whose opinion you trust. Drupal and

WordPress can both be downloaded and installed on your laptop, desktop computer or hosted server space. After comparing the performance of each CMS, you could decide whether one of them is suitable, taking into consideration your available resources, as well as current and future business requirements. You could learn how to develop and manage the CMS yourself, or hire a developer or agency to carry out the work. Understanding at least the basics of using a CMS, such as how to add and edit content, will help you to better evaluate the ways in which using it might benefit your business.

When choosing your hosting package, ensure that the CMS you want to use can be installed, as this might not be possible with some of the cheaper shared hosting packages. You should be able to install WordPress or Drupal onto your hosting space via a web based control panel. The default location for installation is the root folder, although you could choose to install it within a subfolder. Click the Install button and follow the instructions which appear onscreen. When choosing an administrator username avoid using something obvious, such as admin. Use strong passwords, which could include upper and lower case letters, numbers and punctuation characters. The administrator username and password can be used to login to the site after installation, though it is best practice to then set up a different administrator level username and password, to be used for managing your website on a day to day basis.

During the initial CMS setup, select options such as the default language, currency, country, timezone and date format. Enter your contact details, a site email address and give your site a name, for example the name of your business. Although the basic installations of both WordPress and Drupal will include many core features needed by a website, to get functionality not included it will be necessary to download, install and activate or enable the appropriate WordPress plugins or Drupal Modules. When choosing which modules or plugins to use, look for those that are well supported and provide the features you want. For example, modules or plugins could be installed that are designed to increase customer engagement using blogs and forums, provide multimedia content, create custom email messages and thank you pages, or improve site management, performance and security.

Until your website is ready to be launched it should be placed in maintenance mode, so that visitors will only see an under construction page, though you could also display some contact details. You will be able to create user roles with permissions, add content, setup site navigation and configure the CMS as required. When it comes to the visual design of your website you will find thousands of free and paid themes to choose from. They can be downloaded and installed, to change the appearance of your site, though that might result in your site not projecting the unique image you are looking for. If you want your site design to reflect your business brand, then rather than paying a designer to create a theme from scratch, you could select a base theme to configure, though you might benefit from hiring a professional theme designer to do the work for you.

Hosting Your Website

Having your own website will require a physical server that is running the necessary software. A business will generally rent a package from a hosting company, that can manage tasks such as server maintenance, updates and upgrades. This could mean paying for shared hosting, a virtual private server (VPS) or a dedicated server. Shared hosting is the least expensive option and the easiest to set up, though you will be sharing the server with many other sites and have only limited customisation options. It could be suitable for a business requiring a basic website. A VPS is generally more expensive than basic shared hosting. With a VPS you share the server with other websites, but your site will be located within its own partition, making it suitable for sites requiring more advanced features, such as small eCommerce or community sites. The most expensive option is hosting your site on its own dedicated server, suitable for websites with more demanding requirements, such as high levels of traffic and the need for greater control over server management. Hosting packages are typically managed using a browser based control panel.

The company hosting your website could offer you the option of hosting it on either a Linux server or a Windows server. When making your decision, the operating system running on your home computer, such as Mac or Windows, is irrelevant. Linux is an open source operating system and the most widely used on servers hosting websites. Windows Server is a version of the operating system designed to run on servers. When deciding whether to host your website on a server running Linux or Windows, compare their costs and features in relation to your resources and requirements. Linux tends to have lower upfront costs and is a popular choice for those wanting to run open source software, such as PHP and MySQL. Windows has licensing costs and is typically the preferred choice when there are specific requirements, for example the need to run Microsoft based technologies such as ASP.NET.

Before you decide which company to host your website with, think carefully about your requirements and expectations. For example, there are advantages to choosing a company that will host your website on servers running within the country that you are basing your business and where you expect to attract most of your customers. Seek advice from people whose opinion you respect and read online reviews that compare hosting services. Dedicated hosting will usually have a minimum initial twelve month contract, so look for guaranteed Service Level Agreements (SLAs) for things such as uptime. If you choose shared or VPS hosting look for a monthly contract, so that you can change to an alternative package or provider if you are not satisfied with how it performs. A typical hosting package will include hard disc space, within which to store website files, bandwidth, which is the amount of data that can be uploaded or downloaded, some form of technical support and hosted email. Having a professional looking email address, which uses your first name and your own domain name, will add to the credibility of your business and reflect your brand identity.

CHAPTER 7 PRICING YOUR WORK

Pricing Decisions

Regardless of how talented or hardworking a business owner is, if he or she wants to be successful then they must make sales and earn a profit, which means getting the pricing right. However, determining the best price at which to sell their work can be a difficult decision for many people. Pricing requires an understanding of all costs involved in supplying a product or service to a customer, which will then enable the business owner to calculate the price they must charge to break even. In simple terms anything charged above this break even price would be profit and anything sold below this price would be a loss. We will initially look at pricing as it might relate to a business selling any product or service, before considering some factors of particular relevance to an arts and crafts based business.

Cost Price

A business owner should be aware of their overall running costs and what they need to charge their customers in order to break even and make a profit. Fixed costs must be paid regardless of the volume of production or sales, whilst variable costs change according to the amount of work produced for sale. Consequently having fixed costs that are too high could become a problem if the level of production and sales are too low. Increases in variable costs should be covered by growing sales revenue. Some costs will be applied to each item sold, but others will be spread across a number of sales. You should ensure that you understand how money within the business is being spent and you are getting good value.

Calculate the cost per unit by adding together all of your fixed and variable costs and dividing this amount by the number of items produced. When running a business you should look for ways to reduce costs and increase profits, by finding competitive advantages in purchasing and pricing strategies. For example you could increase production and buy materials in bulk, which will often attract a discount, reducing per unit costs. However, you should avoid being left with too much unused materials or unsold stock, as this will impact on your cash flow and tie up money that could instead be used to promote growth.

Sales Costs

There will be costs associated with putting your work in front of customers and selling to them and you should take these into account when pricing your work. If you are an artist or maker selling work to shops, who then sell it on to their customers, this should be considered in your pricing. For example, if production and packaging costs an average of twenty pounds or twenty dollars per unit, then you might sell what you make to a high street store for a price of forty per unit. The retail price charged by the store might then be eighty, in order to cover their costs and leave them with a profit.

If you sell directly to customers, this can remove the need to pay someone else for selling your work. You could then charge customers the full retail price. However, you should consider the costs associated with selling your work, perhaps online through your own website, or in person at a craft fair. Unless payments are made in cash, there would be transaction fees, such as when customers make payments using a credit card or PayPal. Your will need to decide whether increased turnover will cover any extra costs and provide you with sufficient profit.

Price Testing

Through a process of price testing you could try to find the so called sweet spot, where the price you set achieves the greatest volume of sales at the highest price and delivers the maximum profit. This could be determined using market research and trying to sell your work at various price levels, so that you can compare the number of sales and overall profit earned. For example when attending different crafts fairs, you could vary the prices you charge for items that you sell and then compare the resulting profits from each event. You might find that on average people who visit particular events held at certain venues or locations are prepared to pay either more or less than those attending other events. Your findings could help to establish how much you are able to sell your work for and where you might find your best customers.

Selling Price

To achieve sufficient profit from each sale, you should set an appropriate selling price. Some businesses have a large turnover but fail to make a profit, because their costs are too high or their prices are too low. By comparison another business with a smaller turnover could be earning a healthy profit, by keeping their costs low and getting their pricing right. If your prices are too high then you could suffer from a lack of sales. Setting your prices too low would reduce potential profits and might lead to losses. Either approach could become unsustainable and lead eventually to business failure.

As a business owner you should know what your customers are prepared to pay for a particular product or service. You should therefore ensure that you understand the market for the work that you will be selling. Visiting appropriate shops and attending crafts fairs or exhibitions, will allow you to see what others are charging for similar work. When setting your own prices, try to remain competitive, without underselling or competing purely on price. Do not make the mistake of trying to compete with a business that is charging too little. You need sufficient profits to manage cash flow and run a successful business.

Premium Pricing

Rather than competing only on price, you should differentiate yourself through the quality of your work and the level of service that you provide. Establish a reputation as an artist or craft maker creating work of superior quality, which is worth the prices that you charge. Having calculated your available budget and what you believe customers will be prepared to pay, purchase the best tools and materials that your budget will allow. Use the skills that you have learned to make work that is original, of superior quality and designed to appeal to your target audience. Have confidence in your work and believe it is worth the price you are selling it for. Trust that when you find the right customers they will appreciate what you have created and pay the asking price.

Although you should aim for the premium end of the market, do not overcharge your customers. When people pay premium prices, they will expect work of superior quality. You charge more because you take a pride in your work, you don't cut corners and you maintain high standards. High prices will support the use of the best tools, expensive materials, original designs and superior production techniques. It will also provide the resources needed to effectively manage and promote your business and sufficient profit margin to invest in future growth. There is a cost associated with attracting each new customer and you might earn more money overall from a few higher paying customers, rather than a larger number of customers who each spend less. Having a large customer base could also increase the administrative workload, though it should reduce the potential risks of depending on a small number of clients.

Premium Branding

When purchasing commodity items based upon their functionality and usefulness, people are generally price conscious and will look for the best deals available. This means that they might change brands when they find another business selling a similar product for less money or with features that they prefer. However, when an item is designed to appeal to their sense of style and prestige, people tend to value perceptions of brand quality, desirability and exclusivity. This is why people are prepared to pay a premium when purchasing fashionable designer products that are used by role models and inspire respect among their peer group. Limited availability, luxury packaging and celebrity endorsements can increase the appeal of an item and support higher prices than similar products that are not as sought after.

Although you might have limited resources, you can still apply to your own business some of the methods used by well known brands. Understand your target audience and reflect in your marketing and communications the lifestyle that they aspire to. As an artist or craft maker the work that you create should appeal to the taste and aesthetic preferences of your customers. When people are treating themselves or looking for a special gift, they will often be prepared to pay more for luxury items and you can fulfil that demand by creating unique work of superior quality. Having a clearly defined brand identity which appeals to your audience, could attract a loyal customer base. Through word of mouth and association with people who are lifestyle and thought leaders, your work could become more desirable to discerning buyers.

Customer Demand

There is often a greater cost involved in marketing your work to new customers rather than attracting people who have previously bought from your business. Appealing to existing customers could therefore be a sensible way of spending some of your marketing budget. For example a loyalty scheme could offer incentives to those making repeat purchases, such as limited edition exclusive items or invitations to exhibitions of your work. You could send good customers free samples of new product ranges that you are working on and request their comments, reviews and testimonials. People who buy your work could begin to invest in it emotionally and proudly show it to other people, who might in turn become customers.

Think about ways in which you can differentiate what you do and try to identify unmet demand or a profitable niche that you can fill. When positioning yourself and what you sell in the market, you could be competing with other artists and makers based not just in your own region or country, but around the world. You might find that demand for your work begins to exceed your capacity to create it, whilst maintaining the required quality. At this point you could increase the prices that you charge, until demand drops to a level you can cope with. Alternatively, if it is appropriate to do so, you could employ other artists or makers to create work according to your designs. Although this might change the nature of your business, it could enable you to supply a larger market, increase turnover and increase profits.

Discounting

You might be tempted to reduce prices in order to increase sales. However, your cost price will remain the same. Therefore a small percentage discount in the price that you charge customers, will result in a larger drop in the percentage of profit that you receive from each item sold. Consequently if sales growth does not make up for this reduced margin, your overall profits will fall. Providing a discount could also reduce the perceived value of your work. This might attract customers who are looking for a bargain, rather than those who are prepared to pay for superior quality products and services. Never cheapen the perceived value or quality of your work by appearing to be desperate to sell it for less than it is worth. However, if you have excess unsold stock and want to clear space for new stock, then you could sell some items at a discount for a limited period and perhaps make the offer available to selected customers.

Multiple Income Streams

Developing multiple income streams can reduce the potential risks associated with depending upon only one source of revenue. However, this might lead to a loss of focus on essential activities, the spreading of resources too thinly or an increased workload that could become overwhelming. This could affect the delivery of the main products or services from which a business generates most of its revenue. A situation could arise though in which a business is no longer able to generate sufficient profits from the sale of existing products or services, when sold at the prices it is able to charge. When a business is struggling financially, it might also lack the resources required to research and develop new sources of income.

When a business is in a good financial position, it might be sensible to carry out some market research. This could identify new opportunities and unmet customer demand. Rather than waiting until it reaches a growth plateau or slump in sales, a business could invest in the development of new products or services, as part of its long term strategy. Ideally these new income streams would complement existing business activities and branding. This additional income could support business growth and reduce the risks associated with loss of market share due to increased competition or seasonality. For example an artist or maker might decide to learn additional skills, develop a new creative style, organise craft fairs or begin running a course or workshop.

CHAPTER 8 SELLING IN PERSON

Buyers and Sellers

Some people are happy to search for and purchase items online, in part because they enjoy the convenience and comfort of doing so from their own home, while other buyers prefer to see an item in real life before parting with their money. You should consider this when promoting a piece of artwork or handmade craft online, as the aesthetic appeal is of greater importance than with commodity purchases, such as general household goods. Customers purchasing handmade items, often do so because they appreciate the high quality and uniqueness of each piece. Established artists and makers might display and sell their work through a studio, gallery or shop, where members of the public can see their work and possibly meet them. However, the first experience that many people will have of selling in person work that they have created, is when they book a stall at a craft fair.

When customers buy premium items, they expect to receive a superior level of customer care. For example if you have met someone previously, they might be more likely to make a purchase if you can recall their name and any preferences that they told you about. This appeals to our human desire for exclusivity and to feel valued as individuals, reflecting the difference between basic essentials which people expect to be inexpensive compared to luxury items and gifts, for which people are prepared to pay more. Therefore regardless of how wonderful your work might be, you are more likely to be successful if you communicate effectively with customers. Meeting the person who created a piece of work, can add to the sense of authenticity and could lead to additional sales. By engaging with their customers in person, artists and makers can also receive direct feedback about their work. This could help to boost their confidence, motivate them and attract commissions for bespoke work.

Sales Skills

There are common misconceptions surrounding what makes a person good at sales, such as their being loud, aggressive and ruthless. However, in order to be successful over the long term a business needs to attract loyal customers who will happily make repeat purchases. This requires the seller to find the best prospects when seeking new customers and building a successful relationship with their clients, that is based upon mutual trust and reciprocal benefits. In addition to knowledge of the product or service they are selling, good salespeople have excellent communication skills, ask the right questions, listen to the answers they receive and understand their customers wants and needs.

Some people wrongly assume that being able to sell is an inborn characteristic, but it is a skill and can be learned through suitable training. It is also sometimes said that a good salesperson can sell anything to anyone. In reality success in sales requires an understanding of what you are selling and being able to find the appropriate customers, which highlights the importance of effective market research. People buy a product or service because they believe it is going to improve their life or help them to achieve an objective. When a purchase fulfils their expectations, they are more likely to feel motivated to buy again and pass on recommendations to family, friends and colleagues.

Arts and Crafts Fairs

Each year thousands of arts and crafts fairs are held at venues ranging from school and church halls, with a few dozen stall holders and mainly local visitors, to large indoor or outdoor events, attracting hundreds of stallholders and thousands of visitors. You might prefer to begin at a small local event, in order to gain some experience and build your confidence, before showing your work at a large event. When you sell work directly to customers at an event, you need to determine whether the potential increase in sales will make the extra expense worthwhile. Consider factors such as the costs involved in exhibiting at a particular event, the items other stall holders are selling and the audience that the event is expected to attract. Before booking a stall, estimate the potential return on your investment in terms of the opportunity to market your business and increase sales, both on the day and longer term.

Finding Suitable Events

When you are looking for events at which to sell your work, it is worth while researching possible venues and understanding what you could do to increase the prospects of success. You could begin by seeking recommendations from other people, looking online for websites that promote events and reading relevant publications. Visiting a few events will provide you with an opportunity to explore each venue, judge the range and quality of work on sale and evaluate how well the event is run by the organisers. In addition to forming your own impressions, you could politely ask stallholders for their thoughts about the event. Without being too intrusive, you could chat to other visitors, gaining some insight into what they are looking for in the items that they buy. You could also ask visitors if they would attend the event again or recommend it to other people and decide whether the audience appears to be the type of people who would purchase what you make.

Finding appropriate events at which to market and sell your work is a crucial part of being successful. Before booking a stall you should therefore ask event organisers relevant questions, such as how they will be promoting the event and whether you may read exhibitor and visitor testimonials from previous events they have run. Organisers should be taking steps to ensure that the number and range of stalls will mean that there is a good variety of arts and crafts items on show. You should ask the organiser how many visitors they are expecting, enabling you to calculate the average cost per customer by dividing this number by the table cost. You can then compare the various events that you have looked at. However, visitor numbers could be affected by unpredictable factors such as the weather. Also whilst some stall holders at an event might sell well, others at the same event could struggle, perhaps because of what they are selling, their pricing or presentation.

When you approach an organiser about booking a stall at one of their events, they will typically ask for a description of your work and to see photographs or a sample of what you make. Many organisers have a strict policy of handmade goods only and this helps them to maintain a high standard of arts and crafts exhibitors at their events. Consider the time of year and any other events taking place in the local area on the same day, which could either reduce visitor numbers or attract more passing trade. Ask the organiser about transport links to the venue and whether there will be adequate parking and accessibility both for stallholders and visitors. Enquire about facilities such as refreshment areas, in addition to the provision of clear directional signposting on the day, to help exhibitors and visitors find the venue.

When a venue is local to you, it will be easier for family and friends to come along on the day to offer support and help out on the stall. If the venue is a considerable distance from home, you should consider the greater travel costs and the possible need to pay for overnight accommodation. Exhibiting at a small event might involve a low table fee, though you should also include the cost of your time and stall presentation materials. Organisers running large prestigious events, will generally incur greater costs for things such as venue hire, staff wages and advertising, resulting in higher table fees and possibly visitor entry charges. However, you should expect this to be reflected in the superior quality of the venue and a prime location could help to attract a good level of footfall on the day, including passing trade. The organiser should have put in place an effective campaign to market the event online and across suitable local or national media.

Some people attend craft fairs to browse for gift ideas or because they like to collect handmade work. Other visitors could be looking for a particular artist or maker, from whom they could have bought items previously and who might have invited them to the event. Trade buyers, such as interior designers, could visit an event looking for unique high quality items that match the taste of their clients. Visitors to more prestigious events might be more likely to pay a premium for superior quality handmade work or decide to commission bespoke items. Such events could prove to be a worthwhile investment, if they can increase your profits, by enabling you to find new customers for your work, who you might not have otherwise met.

Before The Event

Having booked a stall at a craft fair, good preparation could increase the chances of having a successful day. Consider the type of visitors you expect to attend the event and which items you think will sell well. Plan how you are going to pack your work so that it can be safely transported to the event and quickly unpacked when you arrive. Ensure that you have the correct address for the venue, plan the best route to get there and know where you can park your vehicle. Setting up and running a stall will be easier if you invite a friend or relative who can help, particularly at busy events, or if you take a large amount of stock. When attending events on your own, you could get to know other stallholders and keep an eye on each others stalls when taking refreshment breaks. Other useful things to take with you include display stands for your work, a chair, cash box, calculator, and bags, in which customers can carry their purchases, with appropriate packaging materials for fragile items.

Initially you might prefer to book craft stalls at smaller events and sell a few less expensive items in addition to your premium quality work. Decide how you are going to manage customer payments. For small purchases cash transactions are generally acceptable and you could use a petty cash box, though you should keep track of the money and reconcile it at the end of each day. However, for higher priced items many people prefer to pay by credit or debit card, rather than cash or cheque. As your business grows you might therefore decide to get a merchant account, which could reduce the risk of losing potential sales. Ensure that you have the necessary insurance to cover against damage or injury caused by your stall, what you sell, or any equipment you will be using, for example if you are going to demonstrate how your work is made. Event organisers will expect you to have the relevant documents and you should bring proof with you on the day of the event, as the organiser might ask to see them.

Find out what time you can enter the venue and begin setting up your stall. If tables are being supplied, ask for the dimensions and obtain a white tablecloth that is large enough to cover the table top. Allowing the cloth to drop at the front and sides could hide additional stock stored under the table. However, the tablecloth should not be so long that someone could trip over it. A second smaller cloth could be placed in the middle of the table, of a colour that compliments the overall look of your stall. Practice setting up your craft stall at home, to ensure that you have a good table layout and so that you can time how long it takes both to set up and pack away your stall. Ensure your work is displayed so that it can be easily seen from a distance, for example by ensuring that larger items are placed behind smaller items, so as not to obscure them. Also if you are selling items such as pictures or greeting cards, stand them up rather than laying them flat on the table.

The design of your stall should effectively display your work and reflect your business brand. You could seek the assistance of someone with experience arranging stall displays or seek the opinion of people whose taste you respect. Consider the choice of colour scheme, materials and lettering, on everything from display stands, posters, packaging and labels, to leaflets, stationery and business cards. A stall should attract the attention of people passing by, appealing to their sense of taste and style. However, do not upstage the items that you are selling and instead provide a setting that compliments them, perhaps by placing items within an appropriate context. For example vintage items could be placed within a retro looking stall, whilst contemporary pieces would suit clean elegant lines and props could be used with household items such as ceramics. Artists use elements such as size, weight, shape and colour when composing a painting and in a similar way you could consider the relative positioning of each object. Also understand how the available lighting will affect the appearance of your stall.

Prominently position signs stating that all items for sale on your stall were handmade by you, which could be illustrated with photographs of you working. This could be emphasised by having signs made from the materials used in your work, such as wood, metal, textiles or ceramics. Working at your art or craft whilst at your stall could attract the attention of visitors, but discuss this with the organiser prior to the event date. If you need access to power outlets, then confirm whether they will be available near the stall or if extension leads will be required. If there is a wall behind your stall, ask the organiser if you can attach a promotional banner or use display stands. Textile designers wanting to hang clothes they have made could ask if there is space for additional racks or rails. Ensure there is enough room for people to move safely and comfortably around your stall and look at your work. Including an item on your stall that is both impressive and expensive could attract people who might then purchase items within their budget.

The quality of promotional material such as banners and signs used on your craft stall can influence the perception that people have of your business and your work. It is therefore worthwhile investing in a well designed, easy to transport and setup point of sale display. If promotional banners and posters are durable and do not have a specific date or venue printed on them, then they could be reused at other events. Although you could try making promotional materials yourself, you will probably find a local print shop that can produce them at a reasonable cost and of a higher quality. To ensure that everything is consistent with your business branding, you could carry out the design work yourself or oversee the process and then have the files sent, in the appropriate format, to the print company. They might be able to offer you better rates if you order a range of printed material such as branded packaging, brochures, leaflets, stationery and business cards. When selecting a printing company, you might have preferences that reflect your brand, such as finding one that uses recycled materials and eco friendly production processes.

On The Day

Think of your stall as a temporary retail outlet. Arrive at the event early, ready to set up your stall before the doors open and the first visitors arrive. You might have previously visited the venue, requested a table plan and reserved a good stall location. Alternatively if tables are not already allocated by the event organiser, then you might be able to secure a good stall position, providing you with the best opportunity to be seen by and engage with potential customers. If you have previously practiced setting up your stall, then it might help to have a checklist prepared describing each step involved and photographs of the completed stall display. Item prices should be clearly displayed, as although some people will happily enquire how much something costs, others could walk away without asking. Place business cards on the table where they are easy to pick up, along with marketing materials that you would like people to take away with them. Ensure that the stall and its surroundings are safe both for yourself and other people, by for example tidying away any loose cables or boxes that people might trip over.

During The Event

The manner in which you present yourself and the first impression that you make upon potential customers can affect their buying decisions. Make an effort to smile, remaining friendly and approachable as people pass by your stall. Engage with those who show an interest in your work and be prepared to answer any questions they might have. Do not appear unhappy if you are struggling to make sales. Each person you speak to provides an opportunity to carry out some market research, promote you work, get contacts and find potential customers. As an artist or craft maker, you have the advantage of possessing a deep understanding and genuine passion for what you do. However, you should be careful not to get too carried away when talking about your work to potential customers. Listen to what people say, observe their body language, gently persuade and look for buying signals. Appreciate people taking the time to speak to you about your work. When someone expresses a genuine interest in purchasing an item, trying to sell them something different could put them off, unless the alternative is clearly more suitable.

When planning conversations that you might have with customers, you could write a script and rehearse with a friend or family member. However, the script should then be put aside and the sales process must seem natural, allowing you to engage with people in a more relaxed friendly manner. When visitors approach your stall and begin looking at your work, try not to say anything until they make eye contact with you. Smile and ask them a question, such as whether they like the item they are looking at, if there is something in particular they are looking for and whether it is to be a gift for someone else or a treat for themselves. Listen carefully to what people say and respond appropriately, asking suitable questions when necessary, without being too pushy. Understanding a customer can help you to match the items they purchases with their wants and needs. This will make them more likely to feel happy with what they have bought and motivated to buy from you again in the future. They might also recommend your work to other people.

Without being arrogant, have confidence in your work and the prices that you charge. If you do not believe in your work, then why should you expect that anyone else will. When someone asks you questions about your work, you should be able to discuss it with them in a friendly manner, without going into more detail than is necessary or talking for too long. If a customer expresses an interest in purchasing an item, or enquires about the price of any items that do not have a price tag attached, respond appropriately. When a customer indicates that they would like to buy an item, be ready to make the sale, offer to wrap the item and ask if they would like a bag in which they can carry their purchase. Regardless of whether a visitor purchases your work on the day, they should leave your stall with a positive opinion of you and your work. Give customers something with your contact details, such as a business card or free sample, so that they can easily purchase from you again in the future, either online or at another event.

Consider what people will see as they approach and walk past your stall and keep it and the surrounding area clean and tidy. After you have made a sale, replace the item with something similar or rearrange the display as necessary. Between sales, speak to visitors about the event and what they are looking for. This could inspire you to create new work, that people have already indicated they would be interested in buying. Let people know about upcoming events where you will also be showing your work. Add new contacts to your opt in mailing list, after receiving their permission to send them email newsletters, updates about other events you will be attending or new work that you create. During quiet spells, you could talk to other stall holders, asking them about their work, their opinion of the venue and whether they know of other upcoming craft fairs where it might be worth booking a stall. You could also exchange business cards with fellow exhibitors, suppliers or other potentially useful business contacts.

After The Event

Spend some time after running an event reviewing how well it went and whether lessons can be learned. Send emails to the event organiser and any customers or business contacts that you met, thanking them for their support and letting them know about future events you will be attending. Determine if you made a profit on the day and which items brought you the best return. When calculating profit or loss, base it upon overall costs and any sales made on the day or during the following days and weeks, to people you met at the event. As you attend more events, some might prove more successful than others. Also you could benefit from related marketing efforts and attract more sales as people become increasingly familiar with your work.

Commissioned Work

When creating your own work, without any restrictions from other people, you have the freedom to seek inspiration and express your personal creativity. However, you might at some point be offered the opportunity to work for a client on a commission basis. Although it can be flattering to be approached by a client who wants to pay you to make something for them, carefully consider what is on offer before agreeing to take on a commission. First you must ask yourself if you are prepared to give up some of your artistic freedom in order to work within a brief from a client. You must also communicate with the client effectively, to ensure that you both understand what is expected and if necessary put it in writing, to avoid later misunderstandings. The client might allow and indeed want you to use your talents as an artist or craft maker to create something original that will impress them. However, you should not make assumptions or change what you have agreed with the client, unless you have good reason to do so, discuss it with them first and receive their written approval.

The questions you should ask potential clients include; whether they have commissioned work in the past, how that went and whether other people will also be involved in the decision making process. Ensure the client understands the type of work you can create and that it is what they are looking for, by for example showing them a range of your previous work and asking for their opinion regarding what they like or dislike. Although you should expect to meet with the client at agreed points as the work progresses and welcome their constructive input, you will probably not want them to micromanage every detail or continually add new change requests. To cover your upfront costs of committing to a commission, you should require an advance payment of perhaps one third, before beginning work, which will not be refunded if the client cancels the commission. Having both agreed upon the terms and conditions of a commission, a contract should be signed, though you might prefer to seek legal advise to ensure that the contract provides you with the necessary legal protection.

Although you might need the money, some jobs can cost you more in terms of time and stress than they are worth. If a client is rude, unreasonable, never satisfied or you do not believe that the commission can be completed as they require, then be prepared to politely turn them down. Accepting the wrong commissions from unsuitable clients, might prevent you from taking on other more lucrative opportunities, with clients that would be a better fit in terms of personality and expectations. Some clients could have had bad experiences with previous commissions and approach you with negative expectations and you should not place yourself in the position of being blamed for the failures of others. However, if you find yourself in such a situation and are able to reach or even exceed client expectations, then they might be so impressed that they offer you more work or recommend you to other people.

Remember that clients are paying for your experience and expertise as an artist or craft maker. Therefore if you express a lack of confidence in your work, clients could begin to doubt their decision to hire you and decide to look elsewhere. Be realistic regarding the amount of time needed to complete a commission, rather than over promising and then delivering the work late. Without being arrogant or dismissive, be prepared to disagree with the ideas that a client puts forward, if you believe they are wrong and you can offer them better alternatives. The client might be unsure of what they are looking for and welcome your advice. Maintaining a cordial but professional relationship with your clients should help you both to manage challenges that could arise while you are working on a commission. Ultimately the experience should be positive for you both and result in a piece of work that your client is happy with and that you are proud to put your name to.

CHAPTER 9 SELLING ONLINE

Purchasing Decisions

When selling person to person in the real world, as you might in a shop or at a craft fair or exhibition, customers can see and touch your work. You can also develop rapport with them and look for buying signals. However, when selling online you rely on the ability of your website to engage effectively with customers, so that they are motivated to make a purchase. You should therefore ensure that the quality of the images and descriptive text that you upload are a good representation of your work. In addition to practical considerations, our purchasing decisions are influenced by how something makes us feel. The use of appropriate images can help to communicate some sense of the aesthetic qualities of an item, whilst text can answer questions and provide information that could lead to a sale. Emotional response is particularly important with luxury items and gifts, such as handmade arts and crafts, where aesthetics are likely to be of a greater priority than when comparing the practical benefits of everyday essentials.

Sales Platforms

Having a presence online is generally considered to be an important part of running a business in the twenty first century. Your website and social media activities should support business branding and marketing, providing information about your products or services and enabling customers to easily contact you. When deciding to promote and sell your work online, you could do so through your own website, a hosted service or by registering for an account with an online marketplace, such as eBay, Etsy or Amazon. The path that you decide to follow will depend upon your resources and requirements.

Before deciding which approach to take, read reviews and seek advice from other people. You could try promoting and selling your work on a few different platforms and compare the performance of each, or invest in your own eCommerce website. Based upon a comparison of how well you believe each platform will meet your requirements and having read any relevant terms and conditions, you should be better able to make an informed decision as to which platform to use.

Marketplace Platforms

When you register for an account to sell your work through one of the online marketplace platforms, you should be able to get up and running relatively quickly. Typical costs associated with having such a marketplace shop could include a monthly or annual subscription, a fee to list each item or a charge when items are sold. The provider of the service will generally include software tools for the setup and management of your shop, so that you can upload product images, descriptive text, pricing, shipping details and other relevant information. They will provide some form of shopping cart and payment processing options, so that your customers can purchase your work. There might also be the option to apply some basic branding, for example your logo and preferred colour scheme. However, the nature of such shared platforms means that there will often be limits placed upon the functionality and design that you are able to apply.

One of the benefits of using an established marketplace to sell your work is that they can attract huge numbers of users, who are already familiar with how the platform works. However, you will be competing with other sellers for the attention of buyers and success will require an investment of time and resources into the promotion of your shop. When choosing a marketplace platform, consider the expectations of the people using it and whether it will be a suitable place to sell your work. Platforms which are popular with buyers looking for a bargain and sellers offering mass produced items might not appeal to the customers that you are trying to attract. When you are selling handmade arts and crafts, you should look for a platform that attracts visitors who appreciate and are prepared to pay a premium for such work.

Hosted eCommerce

If you intend selling a large number and range of items and want options not available within a marketplace platform, then you might decide to use hosted eCommerce. You would typically pay a monthly fee to the company hosting eCommerce software on their servers, though you should be able to use your own domain name. The hosting company will look after the management of the software platform, handle upgrades and provide you with design templates and user interface tools. Following store setup, you should then be able to focus on content such as product images, descriptive text and the marketing of your work, rather than worrying about the technical side of hosting and software management. The benefits of using hosted commerce could include being able to track and record customer orders and interactions, include content such as a blog and having shipping options for items of different sizes and weights that are being sent to different destinations.

eCommerce Website

If you only intend selling a few items, then having an account with one of the marketplace platforms might meet your requirements. Some people start out by selling their work on one of the marketplaces and then move on to having their own website as their business grows. However, if you want to build a large business, with a strong brand identity and sell a wide range of items to many customers, then you could benefit from starting with your own website, running on its own domain name. This might involve the use of a CMS, such as Drupal or Wordpress, for which eCommerce modules and plugins are available. Once installed, configured and activated on your website, they can provide functionality such as a shopping cart, order tracking, customer management, shipping options and integration with payment processing. Creating appropriate categories within your online shop, to which you can then add the items to be sold, will make it easier for customers to find what they are looking for and complete their purchases.

Your website could be developed as business growth requires, rather than trying to switch to your own website from a marketplace shop at a later date. You could include content, functionality or design features that you think will help to promote and grow your business. When running your website on a VPS (virtual private server) or dedicated server, you should apply for an SSL certificate. SSL (Secure Sockets Layer) is a security standard designed to encrypt communications between your website and other computers that connect to it, such as those used by your customers. It is an essential element of setting up an eCommerce website, if you allow people to login to your website or if you intend storing and sharing sensitive data. You are probably already familiar with the padlock that appears alongside the URL in the browser address bar when a website has an SSL certificate. Obtaining an SSL certificate for your website is something that your hosting company should be able to advise you about.

Online Payments

The buying decisions of customers can be influenced by the quality of their online shopping experience and the availability of their preferred payment method. Therefore a well designed shop offering a choice of popular payment options is likely to attract more sales. If you sell your work through an online marketplace, it will typically provide the shopping functionality and integration with a payment processor, such as PayPal. Some marketplaces might also allow buyers to pay using a debit or credit card and charge the seller a fee for each payment processed on their behalf. When a customer has selected an item that they want to buy, they will be taken to some form of checkout, where they can select a payment option and enter the necessary details. The amount due to the seller will generally be deposited into their account after it is confirmed that an item has been shipped. There might be additional delays before the seller receives the funds, depending upon conditions the marketplace applies.

When running your own eCommerce website, provide visitors with a good user experience and offer customers convenient, reliable and secure payment options. PayPal can be integrated with most shopping carts and eCommerce websites built using a CMS such as Drupal or WordPress. When you have a verified PayPal business account, you can begin accepting payments. Customers that click on the checkout button will be taken to the PayPal website, where they can pay using their PayPal account or a credit or debit card. After paying, the customer can be returned to your website, where the ordering process can be completed, before the item is shipped. PayPal charges sellers a fee for each transaction and the payment, less this amount, will be placed in your PayPal account, from where it can be transferred to the bank account that you have linked to your PayPal account.

When selling through your own website, you might be able to increase sales conversion rates by enabling buyers to pay without leaving the site. If you are using an online marketplace, which offers limited payment methods, then you might want to offer your customers additional options. In both cases you could decide that you need the facility to accept credit card and debit card payments from buyers. The three main elements involved in accepting card payments, whether online, over the telephone or in person, are the payment gateway, payment processor and merchant account. When a buyer submits their order payment online, it goes first to the payment gateway and then the payment processor, for authorisation so that the customers card can be charged. For reasons of security, the details of a transaction cannot be sent directly from a website to a payment processor. The merchant account is a type of bank account, which allows you to accept credit card or debit card payments, so that after a transaction is approved the money can be sent to your business bank account.

If you are setting up a new online business, then you might find that the banks you approach are not prepared to provide you with a merchant account. However, if you are selling work through your own website, then an alternative could be to use a service such as PayPal Website Payment Pro. The payment gateway, payment processor and merchant account functionality will then be provided by PayPal. This would allow buyers to pay by PayPal, credit card or debit card, without leaving your website. Payment solutions are also available from other companies such as Google and Amazon. Although the additional fees charged to sellers could make such services more expensive than having your own merchant account, they should be easier to implement and many buyers will already be familiar with them.

When you enable your customers to pay using credit cards or debit cards, you might be using a hosted solution, so that none of the card data is collected, stored, processed or transmitted within your eCommerce system. However, if you are going to be handling card data on your website and within your business, then you will need to be PCI DSS (Payment Card Industry Data Security Standard) compliant. The global standard exists to increase security around card transactions. You should verify how the regulations have been implemented in the jurisdiction where you do business and what you must do to be compliant. Validation is performed annually either by an appropriate external assessor or, if your business handles only a small number of transactions, by completing a self-assessment questionnaire. When deciding which online payment solutions to offer your customers, you should read the relevant terms and conditions carefully, considering the associated costs and any additional requirements or work involved. Seek advice from people who have the necessary expertise and contact the relevant organisations with any questions that you might have.

Conversion Funnels

Every business that sells a product or service online has a conversion funnel, even if they are not aware of the fact. Within eCommerce, conversion funnels are frequently used to evaluate the performance of a website with regards to the advertising and sales process. They can provide a way for you to visualise the path that a potential customer might follow when finding and visiting your website. However, the concepts involved could be applied more broadly, when evaluating your online or offline business activities. When trying to understand and improve how your business engages with customers, you could also make use of AIDA, which stands for awareness, interest, desire and action, and is covered in the next chapter.

Even the best implemented conversion funnel can lose potential customers at each stage. Typically only a small percentage of people will move from initial awareness of or interest in a product or service to the stage where they complete an action, such as making a purchase. However, a business that has an underperforming conversion funnel could be losing customers to their competitors, without realising why. This could be because they are attracting the interest of people who are not within their target audience, lack of appropriate content, providing a poor user experience, inadequate calls to action or being unresponsive to enquiries. You can analyse each stage, from potential customers becoming aware of what you do, to them first visiting your website and completing a particular action. For example an eCommerce website might have an unfocused marketing strategy, inadequate product descriptions, poor images or a confusing checkout process and too few payment options. Because potential customers can be lost during each stage of a transaction, having fewer steps could also increase the percentage of sales conversions.

When planning your sales and marketing strategy, the use of a conversion funnel can help you to deploy your resources more effectively. You could begin by understanding the current conversion funnel for you business, perhaps by drawing a diagram of the process on a piece of paper or using suitable software. If you are running analytics software on your website, look at the traffic data to gain a better understanding of visitor demographics, how people find your site, which pages they visit and the conversion process. You could identify and address issues that might be causing visitors to abandon the conversion funnel. This should be an ongoing process, rather than a one off strategy. Over time you could begin to see improvements at each stage of the customer journey, leading to more people completing the desired actions. You could develop a number of increasingly detailed conversion funnels, perhaps with segmented marketing campaigns and different paths suitable for new or returning visitors. When there are multiple potential objectives and calls to action, you could include alternative paths for those who abandon a particular funnel.

Calculate the average cost to you of potential customers arriving on your website, as a result of the various forms of advertising and marketing that you are using. Then look at how well they each convert into paying customers, so that you can direct resources towards the approach that brings the best returns. Understand your target audience, so that you can raise awareness with them, rather than spending time and money attracting people who are not interested in your products or services. Many people will visit a website a number of times before making a purchase, therefore you should look for ways to maintain engagement with them. Offering visitors a free newsletter subscription in return for their name and email address could generate leads and an effective series of autoresponder emails might help to increase engagement between buyer and seller. When people abandon the funnel, you could ask them to complete a short survey, with questions designed to help you learn why they have done so and where you might be able to make improvements.

The conversion funnel could also be represented using the terms Top of the Funnel (TOFU), Middle of the Funnel (MOFU) and Bottom of the Funnel (BOFU). At the top of the funnel there are many people who could be attracted to your website, but you want to be found by those who are within your target audience and in the market for what you offer. You could do this by having good quality content on your website, providing information that your audience is looking for and which is also rich in keywords to attract search engine traffic. When they reach the middle of the funnel, potential customers are deciding whether to make a purchase and you need to provide the information that supports a decision to buy from you, rather than a competitor. Finally at the bottom of the funnel, to ensure that a customer purchases the product or service from you, provide a reliable user friendly buying process. Regular evaluation of your conversion strategy, could help you to find opportunities to improve performance.

Packaging and Postage

Customer who have purchased items should receive them within a reasonable amount of time and undamaged. Therefore you should put in place an affordable, efficient packaging and delivery process. Clearly state postal charges and whether for example orders above a certain value include free delivery. Use a box that is slightly larger than the item to be packaged, so that it can be wrapped in protective bubble wrap or paper, but not so large that you waste money on excessive packaging or postage costs. Ensure items are held securely in place and do not move when the package is handled. Place within the box any necessary paperwork, along with the delivery and return address. You could include thank you notes, promotional material or free samples of your other work, which might encourage future sales. Seal the box with strong tape, reinforcing box seams with extra tape if necessary, to ensure the package does not open during transit. Attach a label with the full correct delivery address and include your return address, which should both be clearly printed in easy to read text.

The growth of online shopping has led to consumers expecting convenience and flexibility, both in their experience of buying online and the speed of delivery. Customers often want delivery to be available same day, next day or within a few days, although some will wait longer if free shipping is included with their purchase. If you are running a small businesses, you could struggle to compete with the large online retailers, who might offer a wider range of payment and delivery options than you are able to, such as click and collect. However, you can try to provide a more personalised and responsive customer service experience. Ensure that you have a sufficient stock of packaging and postage supplies to meet demand. Compare the companies offering parcel delivery services, to find one which best meets your requirements at a competitive rate. When deciding which delivery service to use, consider factors such as pickup options, tracking, delivery confirmation and insurance. Ensure that the postage paid for each package you send is correct for the destination.

Suitable packaging materials can be purchased online and supplies such as labels, bags and boxes could be branded with your logo, colour scheme and messaging. The quality of packaging will reflect upon your business and if well designed can help to inspire confidence in the standard of your work. For many people the unboxing experience influences the value they attribute to their purchases. This is reflected in the popularity of online videos showing people unboxing a wide range of products. Unlike a real world retail space, when you are selling online the packaging decisions that you make could be one of the few opportunities that a customer has to physically interact with your business brand. When selling your work person to person, the quality and presentation of your packaging will also form part of the aesthetic experience, which is particularly important with handmade premium quality work. The customer experience should be positive and something people feel motivated to share with others. For example they might decide to post photographs or videos of imaginative packaging to social media, helping to promote your brand and attract more customers.

CHAPTER 10 MARKETING YOUR BUSINESS

What is Marketing?

Marketing describes a range of activities carried out in order to communicate with a target audience and is typically done to raise awareness of a product or service. For a business it might have the objective of promoting a brand and increasing loyalty with existing customers or attracting new customers. When planning a marketing strategy, a business should have an understanding of the audience they are trying to reach and how to engage with them effectively. They should be able to explain the benefits of a product or service and how it will fulfil customer needs or desires. The techniques used in marketing can vary across different media, but to be effective they all require some understanding of psychology, which drives human behaviour and decision making.

Advertising and Public Relations

Advertising and public relations (PR) both fall within marketing, however it can be helpful to define what we mean when using each term. Marketing describes all of the processes involved in the research, planning and delivery to an audience of information that is intended to achieve an objective and the measurement of the results. Advertising is the part of the marketing process in which an advert created to communicate a message is placed within media such as television, magazines, newspapers, radio, billboards and online. Public relations involves the managing of how an individual or organisation is perceived by other people, so as to develop and maintain their good reputation. It can include activities such as writing press releases, arranging interviews, social media engagement and running events.

Across traditional broadcast and print media, large organisations can outspend smaller competitors, who could struggle to get their message noticed. However, a small business with a limited budget, but good ideas, can compete on a more level playing field when advertising and public relations are carried out online. They might be able to develop novel and entertaining campaigns which tell their story and promote their work. This could form the basis of a public relations strategy, attracting free coverage within online publications, broadcast and print media. This also has the benefit that audiences are often more likely to believe an article or story, rather than a piece of paid advertising.

AIDA

The acronym AIDA, which stands for awareness, interest, desire and action, can be used to describe the stages involved in an audience journey, for example when people respond to a message, engage with some form of content or go through the process of buying something. To apply AIDA successfully within your business, you should understand the wants and needs of your target audience and effectively communicate to them that what you are promoting can meet their wants or needs. Awareness requires your target audience to notice your message or piece of content and might result from advertising, word of mouth, social media engagement or online search results. Employing good design and placing your message or content in a suitable location can increase the potential for it to be noticed. Interest could mean that having noticed your message or content, potential customers decide it is relevant to them and if sufficiently motivated to learn more, they could for example visit your website to find additional information.

Desire for what you are selling, involves you convincing people that a product or service can fulfil their needs by focusing on the benefits that will be available to them, if they choose to purchase your product or service. Desire represents something that people are looking for, which appeals to their personal interests and preferences, and which is available with the product or service that you are selling. You should ensure that what you are promoting compares favourably with alternatives available from your competitors, by for example offering premium quality or special features. Action requires the visitor to complete the action that you want them to, such as buying the product or service that you are selling, subscribing to a newsletter or completing a survey. Make it easy for customers to do something, such as making a purchase, by removing possible barriers. For example you could provide clear instructions and an easy to follow path, taking customers to a page on your website which offers convenient payment and delivery options.

Interruption Marketing

For many years various forms of interruption marketing have been used to carry out the mass promotion of products and services. Examples of interruption marketing include television and radio commercials, advertisements appearing in magazines and newspapers, telephone marketing, direct mail campaigns and unsolicited emails. Each involves interrupting what potential customers are doing and drawing their attention towards the marketing message. Although when investing sufficient resources into such an approach businesses can get themselves noticed quickly, the effectiveness of interruption marketing has been reduced by the information overload that people have to deal with in the modern world. Also many people find such interruptions annoying and will do what they can to bypass, ignore or block them. Attempts are often made to segment markets and target messages towards particular audience demographics, who might be more receptive to them. However, they generally lack the personalisation that is increasingly expected in modern forms of marketing and are in competition with the widespread use of mobile devices and choice of available content.

When running a marketing campaign, a business might use interruption marketing to first attract the attention of new potential customers and then try to engage with them on a more personal level. However, television and radio advertising is beyond the budget of most small businesses and is more likely to be used by larger organisations that are trying to reach a regional, national or even international audience. Also there is increasing regulation to control the use of unsolicited telephone, email and direct marketing and their intrusive nature can risk damaging the reputation of a business. There are situations though when you could decide to use print advertising. For example if you want to attract visitors to a local craft fair, let people know about a course that you are running, or to promote an exhibition of your work. This could take the form of an advert in a newspaper, magazine or directory. You could use posters or point of sale displays in locations such as arts and crafts events that you are attending and leaflets could be distributed by hand.

Permission Marketing

The growth of social media platforms and advances in communications technology, have made organisations increasingly aware of the need to engage more directly with their customers and in a more personalised way. This has led to the increasing use of permission marketing, in which people can choose whether or not to receive communications. The use of demographic and other data to customise messages, means that they should more closely match the preferences of those receiving them. Consequently messages about a product or service are more likely to receive a positive response and are less likely to be considered either irrelevant or annoying. Examples of Permission Marketing include opt-in email, in which a person joins a mailing list in order to receive a newsletter, or when someone decides to follow, like or subscribe to an individual or organisation on a social network such as Twitter, Facebook or YouTube. The benefits of permission marketing, when compared to interruption marketing, include the more targeted use of resources, increased engagement and higher customer conversion rates.

Having employed a broad range of marketing strategies to first attract potential customers to their website, a business could then offer free subscriptions to an online tutorial or newsletter. People could then be sent a series of automated emails, called auto responders, during the subsequent days and weeks. The messages could be written to entertain and inform rather than being a sales pitch, which might cause people to unsubscribe. Online surveys could also be created, with questions designed to learn more about customers and their preferences. This could include demographic data such as age, gender, education, social class, marital status and occupation. The greater relevance of messages sent to each person, based upon data they have supplied, could enable a business to better anticipate and meet customer expectations. This could establish greater credibility and trust with customers, increasing engagement, conversion rates and brand loyalty. The data required to implement a permission marketing strategy could be managed using Customer Relationship Management (CRM) software.

Unique Selling Point

When advertising a product or service, the term unique selling point (USP) refers to the essential feature which can be used to differentiate it from a similar product or service sold by competitors. The feature should convey to potential customers a benefit which is both unique and desirable. A slogan that effectively communicates the USP of a business, can help it to be noticed and remembered by customers. If you are unsure what the USP should be for your business, you could carry out a survey to identify what customers consider to be important factors in their buying decision. Then list any of those features that you offer and select the one that your competitors cannot easily replicate. Having a clearly defined USP that can be easily communicated in advertising and marketing messages can help a business to develop a strong brand identity.

Unique Experience Point

It has become increasingly difficult for businesses to establish a USP and many organisations and individuals have begun looking at the unique experience point (UEP) as a way of engaging more effectively with their customers. UEP involves developing strategies related to how a product or service makes the buyer feel, rather than focusing solely on the functional benefit of the USP. The UEP requires a long term process of engagement, beyond the purchasing transaction, taking account of customer preferences and the way that a product or service reflects their sense of self and lifestyle aspirations. Providing the personal touch is one of the great strengths of a small business, compared to larger more anonymous organisations. Customers like to feel valued and appreciated and if you are also able share with them an inspiring vision for your business, then they might want to feel part of your journey. Attracting new customers can be time consuming and expensive, whilst investing in relationship building with existing customers could strengthen their loyalty and potentially lead to increasing numbers of repeat sales.

The UEP has particular relevance to artists and craft makers. Customers who purchase handmade items, are often motivated by aesthetics, appreciate the skill required to create such work and attach greater value to unique pieces compared to mass produced objects. This provides you with an opportunity to share stories about your creative process on social media, which could open up a dialogue with people who might go on to purchase work from you. You could also write a blog about what you do, posting photographs that depict each stage from selecting materials to completing a piece of work. Engaging directly with your customers and responding to their questions, could make you more responsive to their wants and needs. You could send personalised thank you messages when customers make a purchase and let them know about craft fairs or exhibitions at which you will be showing your work and where they can meet you. Without being too intrusive, you could also offer good customers the option of receiving a card with a friendly message or free gift on special occasions, such as birthdays or anniversaries.

Personality Types

Decision making can be influenced by factors including demographics, beliefs, relationships with family and friends, preferences, expectations, ambitions and past experiences. The personality type of an individual can also affect the way in which they perceive and respond to a given message, on both an intellectual and an emotional level. Common personality types include bold, sociable and analytical and most individuals will possess an element of each. People with bold personalities tend to be competitive, driven by results and will look for information that enables them to make a quick decision. They want clear answers to their questions and proven solutions to problems. Analytical personalities will look for the data to support a proposed solution to a problem. They are less demonstrative and will want to take their time considering the available information before they make a decision. Sociable personalities are more likely to be team players, who value relationships and seek creative solutions to a problem. They respond better to a vision and the way in which a solution to a problem will affect people, rather than just the facts and figures.

Psychology and Behaviour

The decisions that we make are influenced by how our brain processes information and it often does so in ways that we are unaware of. This occurs when we learn skills so deeply that we can carry them out without the need to consciously recall each step of the process involved. Classical or Pavlovian Conditioning, discovered by Ivan Pavlov, involves a subject learning to associate some stimulus in their environment, such as the ringing of a bell, with something previously unconnected, such as a physiological change, emotion or behaviour. There are many examples of advertisers using conditioned responses to influence how people feel about their products, by associating them with something or someone that their customers already like, such as a favourite song, famous person, popular event or aspirational lifestyle choice. Marketing professionals devote a considerable amount of time and effort to learning about such principles of human psychology and understanding how they can be applied to the marketing of products and services.

If you are running a small business, with a limited advertising budget, some of the strategies employed by marketing professionals might help to increase your sales. For example, people like to feel that they are part of a select group and having items that are available exclusively to your best clients might help to fulfil this desire. This is one of the reasons that luxury brands often have long waiting lists. When you are pleasant to someone they are more inclined to respond in kind, so for example sending a customer an unexpected gift, can help to increase their customer loyalty, making future purchases more likely. As a species our curiosity makes us keen to investigate something that attracts our attention, so an intriguing title or tagline can make us want to learn more. Words also carry powerful meaning and associations, so you should use them appropriately within your content, for example unique, authentic, original, traditional and handmade reflect qualities valued in arts and crafts.

Human beings process images faster than text, therefore a customer buying decision will have been influenced by presentation and design before they read a description of what you are selling. There is disagreement and ongoing research into the possible effects of particular colours on our emotional state and perceptions can differ between cultures. However, people have reported that shades of blue can make them feel calm or sad, whilst orange creates a feeling of warmth and red stimulates intense emotions. The decisions that we make are often shaped more by our emotional responses than our intellect. This is why many premium brands will devote considerable time and resources into creating feelings of trust and loyalty within their customers and desire for the products or services they sell. People are more likely to purchase a particular product or service if they perceive it to be of superior quality and when it reflects their sense of self and how they want to live, even if that means paying a premium compared to other similar alternatives.

People can be influenced in their buying decisions by the way that they believe others will regard them, based upon the items they own and the lifestyle choices they make. Individuals might look for approval and support from other people and groups whose opinion they care about. They will also look for reviews and testimonials from their peers, such as social likes or shares. Although we want to feel that we have sufficient choice, we can become stressed when confronted by too many options and will be more likely to make a decision when presented with two or three clear alternatives. The fear that we might miss out something could also encourage a purchase. The use of limited time offers is an example of this, as is limited availability, such as when an event states that there are only a few tickets left or an artist produces limited edition prints. Our fight or flight response can cause impulsiveness, such as when a customer makes an impulse buy if they are looking at a range of items and hear that the shop is about to close.

Branding

A brand is the identity of an individual or organisation as perceived by other people and should communicate core values in a positive way. When you run your own business it is important to establish a strong brand identity, so that your customers understand who you are, what you offer and how they can to relate to you. Think about the personality that you want to project and how you want other people to perceive and respond to it. For example if you met a person that embodied the brand personality of your business would you like them, trust them and want to buy the products or services that they were selling. When a business is establishing its own brand identity, elements that it could look at include the business name, slogan and visual design choices such as the logo, typeface and colour scheme. Marketing can help to position and raise awareness of a brand, by for example identifying the target audience, managing the engagement process and establishing a good reputation.

Consider the design quality of any printed marketing material, along with your website, social media and email communications. First impressions are important and using good design can increase confidence within potential customers that your products or services will be of a similarly high quality. Most small businesses lack the resources of large organisations, who might be able to afford expensive design consultants and branding campaigns. However, a small business can still benefit from having a recognisable visual style, that helps to establish a consistent brand and can be used across all of their online and printed material. If available funds are limited, you might decide to design your own marketing material, but unless you are a skilled designer, you will probably benefit from having the work done by a professional. You might know a freelance designer who can do the work within your budget, your contacts might be able to recommend someone, or you could search online, where a range of design services are available.

Decide whether to develop a brand around yourself as an individual or create a brand identity for your business as a separate entity. With a personal brand, you could tell your story as an artist or maker and establish a reputation based upon your unique talents. Content on your website such as tutorials, messages shared across social media, blog posts and your appearance at events, could represent who you are and what you do. However, a separate business brand might be more appropriate if you have ambitions to expand and eventually take on staff, perhaps giving them directions and instructions to create work according to your designs. You could chose a keyword rich business name, that describes what the business does and represents the image you want to project to the world. This could help to position your business in the marketplace, ensure potential customers know what products or services it supplies and potentially attract relevant search traffic online. Alternatively you could combine your personal name with an appropriate keyword and position yourself as the creative force and inspiration behind a business brand.

Social Interactions

Every day you probably meet people who are potential customers or business contacts. For example someone running a business might be interested in ordering unique handmade luxury items that they can give as gifts to their best customers or as incentives to members of staff. Therefore you should always carry well designed business cards, which could even be made from materials used in your art or craft, such as a small textile sample or piece of wood. Have a well practiced elevator pitch, enabling you to quickly describe your business in easy to understand terms. It is not a sales pitch and should instead briefly explain the main product or service that you sell, the market size and your target audience. It could also state who runs the business and key advantages that differentiate your business from competitors. If you wear or use what you create and give samples to family and friends, then other people who compliment the items could be directed to where they can purchase them. You could also agree with fellow artists and makers to recommend each others work to potential clients.

Press Releases

Mass media can reach a huge audience and many business owners would like to receive free coverage, from local or national newspapers, magazines, television and radio. You might decide to begin sending press releases, which you hope will lead to stories appearing in the media that will help to promote your business brand. However, before contacting any publication or channel, understand the audience they cater to, whether it reaches your target demographic and the type of content that will appeal to them. Having identified suitable publications or channels, find the person you need to contact, getting their name, job title, telephone number and email address. Journalists are often very busy, therefore label the email you send to them as a press release, with a subject line that will catch their attention and be easily understood, prompting them to open it. The first few lines should provide key information and a summary of the story, immediately generating interest and encouraging the journalist to read the whole press release, which would typically be approximately three hundred words long. Include relevant information and photographs, if you have them, that would add to the story.

When developing an idea for a press release, you could think about your work as an artist or craft maker and running a small business. Ask yourself how this could form the basis of a human interest story. You might be exhibiting work at a gallery, setting up a studio, running a craft fair or teaching a course or workshop. Perhaps you have an interesting back story, such as a career change and the path leading to your new creative occupation. Can you tell an inspiring story about the hard work involved in setting up your own business and some of the challenges you have overcome or are still dealing with. A brief outline of your proposed idea could provide context and explain to a journalist why you believe it would appeal to their audience. Follow up your email with a telephone call, in which you could ask the journalist if they received the email and invite them to meet and interview you at a suitable location, such as your studio, an exhibition or a craft fair. Be aware of production schedules and lead times across different print, online and broadcast media.

Measuring Performance

One of the advantages of running Internet based marketing campaigns is that you can use analytics software to measure the effectiveness of online advertising, such as pay per click (PPC). This information can enable you to stop running unsuccessful PPC campaigns and look for ways to improve any that could perform better. The budget could be increased for campaigns that attract good quality traffic to your website, if it then converts into profitable sales. Analytics can be used to view data from and measure the performance of social media marketing, so that resources can be better directed towards achieving objectives such as increasing engagement and conversions. It is also important to know if your print based advertising is being seen by your target audience and returning a profit. To measure the effectiveness of advertising placed within magazines, newspapers, or on posters or leaflets, a promotional code could be included, each identifying a different campaign. When a customer places an order, whether online, over the telephone or in person you could ask them how they found out about your business and perhaps offer some form of incentive to those quoting the promotional code.

CHAPTER 11 CONTENT MARKETING

What is Content Marketing?

Content marketing is the creation and distribution of content for the purpose of attracting and engaging with a target audience, so as to find new customers or retain existing customers. The content could be in the form of text, images, audio or video, delivered using channels such as print based media, broadcast television or radio and the Internet. It might be designed to entertain or inform and should reflect both the brand of the business and the interests of the intended audience. Although the use of content in order to engage with customers dates back over a century, the rise of mass media and the Internet has led to it being used more widely. People often ignore or avoid blatant advertising messages. By contrast the aim of content marketing is not to sell a product or service directly, but rather to provide material that an audience will want to consume. Unlike interruption marketing, in which your message gets in the way of the audience experience, your content becomes the audience experience.

When a business is able to gain greater insight into the preferences of a potential customer, advertising messages can be presented in a more targeted way and as part of the content experience. People are more likely to respond positively when information is communicated to them in an appropriate manner and at a time when they feel receptive. For example you might want to subtly highlight to an audience some of the key benefits of a product or service that you are selling. You could write an article or produce a video, with a narrative in which someone benefits from the unique features it offers or illustrate the way in which it complements their lifestyle. Even if a customer knows you are trying to sell them something, they will often appreciate that you have invested the time and resources required to create content which has informed or entertained them. They might also be open to consuming more of the content that you produce in the future and could decide to share the content with family and friends.

Content Creation and Acquisition

Before beginning the process of creating something, it can be a useful exercise to represent in rough form on paper what you are planning to do. This could provide you with an overview and perspective on how a project might achieve your goals. When producing content such as an article, infographic, video or audio, outlining your ideas on paper can help you to see how the elements will fit together. This will also allow you to imagine the ways in which your intended audience might navigate or experience a finished piece of work, such as a website or piece of graphic design. For example you could use storyboards in video production and wireframes to map the layout of content and navigation within a website. When you are going to record a podcast, you could think about the topics that you want to cover, research relevant facts, outline the structure and write rough versions, before completing the final script. You could also create mood boards to represent the look and feel of a piece of work and experiment with design ideas.

 Having determined your objectives and evaluated the resources that are available for a project, you could begin the creative process, after researching relevant information and studying the intended audience. From this you could put together some initial ideas and perhaps do some brainstorming with other people to come up with an approach that you might follow. Having put together some rough outlines of what you are intending to do, you could seek feedback from a representative audience and refine your ideas based upon what they say. When producing web based content you should consider factors such as usability, stickiness and SEO, by for example including relevant keywords and phrases. Each element of a project should have a clearly defined purpose and contribute towards overall success. Try to avoid wasting time and money on something which you later realise is not suitable. Following the release of a piece of work, you should measure how well it is performing, so that based upon your findings, updates can be implemented when appropriate and future versions improved.

The quality of the content used within your website, social media and marketing campaigns can influence the way in which people perceive your business brand and the products or services that you sell. If you already posses the necessary knowledge, skills and resources, you might decide to create your own content, which could give you greater control over the production of material that is suitable for your target audience. However, you might need to learn additional skills, perhaps by attending courses or watching online tutorials. The process of content creation can be time consuming and could become a distraction from working on other important aspects of your business. Therefore if you have the available budget, you might decide that it is more cost effective to outsource content creation to experienced professionals, such as writers, photographers and videographers. Ensure though that anyone you hire, understands the requirements of your business brand and the type of visitors that the finished content they deliver must appeal to.

In addition to creating content in-house or hiring other people to supply content, you could also use work that is in the public domain. Copyright exists to protect the rights of the creator of an original piece of work, such as a photograph, painting, music, book or film. This allows them to earn money by selling the rights to use their work. Copyright is generally applied for the lifetime of the creator plus a certain number of years. Public domain works are no longer under copyright, because the protection has expired, without being renewed. The work then falls into public ownership and can be used without the need to obtain permission. There is a wide range of material available online that is within the public domain, such as the writings of Shakespeare and compositions by Mozart. However, new work based upon them, such as a film or modern recording, will be protected by copyright.

When using content that you do not own the rights to, you should ensure that the content is either not under copyright or the copyright owner has given you permission to use their work.

The creator of an original piece of work, could decide to release it under a Creative Commons license, allowing them to state which rights they reserve and which they do not. A Creative Commons license does not replace copyright, but would for example allow other people to use and share a piece of work. However, the copyright holder might have attached restrictions regarding the way in which their work can be used, such as for non commercial purposes only, or require the inclusion of an author credit. Millions of pieces of work have been made available under Creative Commons and many can be found online. People using or sharing material released under a Creative Commons license are protected from infringement of copyright, provided they follow the license conditions. However, you should ensure that you are certain of the Creative Commons status of a piece of work before using it within your own content marketing. If necessary, contact the copyright owner to discuss the way in which you want to use their work and obtain their permission before doing so.

The quality and presentation of content within your website and across social media should be designed to attract and gain the interest of your target audience, moving them along a path towards particular actions. The phrase 'content is king' has been widely used in relation to websites for many years and can also be applied to social media. Examples of popular content include; articles about overcoming challenges and achieving success, advice on issues of common concern to your readers, top ten lists, how to guides and tutorials. Whilst public domain or Creative Commons licensed works can provide useful source material, creating something new based upon them could help you to produce content that will more effectively attract and engage with your target audience. However, before posting content on a social media platform, ensure that you are aware of the terms and conditions of the service that you are using. Fair dealing in the United Kingdom and fair use in the United

States, allows limited use of work that is protected by copyright, for example as part of a review, though you should be aware of any restrictions and requirements that apply.

Website Content

During the planning and development stages of a website, resources are often devoted primarily to visual design and technical functionality and whilst these are important, content might not be given sufficient consideration. Content acquisition can be time consuming and expensive, resulting in a situation where a website is approaching launch date, but there are insufficient resources available for the provision of enough good quality content. When content is supplied after a website has been developed, the site design and navigation might get in the way of a good user experience. This could make it more difficult for visitors to consume the content, increasing bounce rates, reducing time spend on the site and lowering levels of engagement. Having fewer and less motivated visitors would likely result in lower conversion rates and lost sales. Therefore when planning your website, you should consider content marketing strategy from the beginning. This will enable you to plan the design and development of your website and choice of blogging and social media platforms around your content, rather than content becoming an issue during and after the launch of the site.

When planning content marketing across your website, think about the path that different visitor types might follow and how they could be feeling at each stage. Try to match content, messages or calls to action with what they are likely to be thinking about at that point. Use analytics software to understand how people find and respond to different content and ask for visitor feedback. Use this information to help you decide if improvements could be made to the layout of web pages and site navigation. People prefer to visit websites that reflect their preferences, therefore the more that you know about your visitors and how they respond to your content the better you can meet their expectations. If content fails to match visitor interest or mood, they are more likely to leave a site and might not return. Regularly updating your website with fresh content could give people a reason to return and might increase visitor engagement. Understanding your audience and relevant trending topics on social media, can help to guide your choice of content and motivate visitors to recommend your site to other people.

Written Content

Well written text will probably form an an important part of your content marketing. In addition to the subject matter and tone being appropriate for the intended audience, you should consider the medium through which it will be delivered. Written content could appear in printed material, such as a brochure, magazine, leaflet or poster, or online within a website, electronic newsletter, blog post or social media. You should consider that people could be doing other things when consuming your content, such as travelling on a train, taking a meal break, watching television or in a social situation. This can influence how much and for how long they will focus on a piece of text. People could easily be distracted by other things, therefore when laying out content you should clearly signpost and highlight major topics and key pieces of information. You should ask other people to proof read what you have written and it should be viewed on a range of different devices.

People typically read text printed on a page in ways that differ from text appearing on the screens of electronic devices. Printed text is often read from start to finish, allowing a writer to build complex ideas and arguments in a sequential way. Printed text is also generally read faster, more information is retained and readers are less likely to experience eye strain. People tend to skim over text displayed on a screen, move around a web page, look at headings and summaries or read ahead and go back to fill in missing details. Readers tend to prefer shorter sentences and shorter paragraphs when text is displayed on a screen, compared to text in printed publications. They are less likely to be prepared to read large blocks of text or focus their attention on screen based text for long periods of time. There is also a greater probability that people will be distracted by other content and decide to visit a different web page or website.

When writing text that will be published online, use relevant descriptive headings, to attract the attention of your target audience. Opening sentences should engage with readers. Make it clear what the subject matter of a story or article is, highlight why people should continue reading and motivate them to do so by maintaining their interest. Write using clear easy to understand language and avoid the use of ambiguous or confusing terminology. If you provide hyperlinks leading readers to additional details or supporting information, then you should ensure that the links work as expected and open the appropriate web pages. If you want people to be attracted to what you have written, provide a good summary, focusing on key details and getting to the essence of your story or article. This summary could then be posted elsewhere on your website, on a different site or social media platform. If you are going to include images such as photographs or infographics, then ensure they are relevant and effectively illustrate the text that you have written.

Writing a Blog

A blog is like a diary, which rather than being private is published online and the writer of a blog is commonly referred to as a blogger. A blog could be hosted on a blogging platform or the bloggers own website. Depending upon the type of business that you are running and the image you want to project, you could create a blog under your own name, or it could be under a business brand name. The visual design of your blog should reflect your work and business brand and the use of descriptive keyword rich blog titles, could help to attract the attention of readers and boost search traffic. During recent years, social networks such as Facebook and Twitter have emerged, which can be used by people to share information about themselves and their lives, where they might previously have written a blog. Social media could however provide an opportunity for you to find and engage with a new audience, who might then decide to visit a blog hosted on your own website, over which you have greater control.

Blog posts typically appear in date order and are often submitted at regular intervals, for example on the same day each week. The content of your blog posts should cover subject matter that you are interested in, have some understanding of and which you believe will appeal to your target audience. You could write about your life and work as an artist or craft maker, describing the process of creating a piece of work and how you select the tools and materials that you use. Other topics could include particular artists and makers who have inspired you, craft fairs and exhibitions that you have attended or some of your experiences and lessons learned setting up and running your own business. Ensure that any details or quotes you include are correct, carrying out additional research if necessary to confirm the accuracy of facts and figures. Look for new and interesting perspectives on a subject, which could include opinions or questions designed to prompt a response from readers. You could also upload photographs and include hyperlinks to supporting audio or video content.

Try to develop a consistent writing style that will engage with your target audience and find your own unique voice through which to express your thoughts. Popular blogs often have a clearly defined identity and cover subjects that appeal to a particular audience. Whilst being friendly and approachable, remain professional and although you could use humour, take care not to upset or offend your readership. For example you could describe personal experiences that other people might be able to relate to, such as an amusing anecdote from an event that you attended. However, you should only share information that you are comfortable revealing and retain your sense of integrity. You could encourage readers to subscribe to your blog and begin posting their own comments or questions, providing you with an opportunity to communicate directly with your audience and build a relationship with them. A well written blog could attract a loyal and engaged readership, helping to establish your reputation and increasing your credibility with potential customers. You might even become respected as a thought leader, inspiring other people with your work and ideas.

Newsletters

A well designed newsletter, featuring content that is timely and relevant, can inform readers about topics of interest to them and appropriate calls to action could prompt a response. Although some organisations continue to publish physical newsletters and deliver them via direct mail, many now prefer the less expensive alternative of sending newsletters via email. However, there is still a considerable investment of time and resources required to publish and distribute a newsletter on a regular basis. Therefore when considering producing a newsletter for your business, you should first ask yourself what your objectives are and whether a newsletter could achieve them. For example do you want to promote your business brand, retain existing clients or attract new clients. Look at popular newsletters and ask yourself if you could produce something of a similar quality. Carry out some market research, to better understand what type of content would appeal to your target audience and decide if you could deliver what they want.

If you decide that a newsletter campaign is an appropriate form of marketing for your business, plan how you are going to achieve your objectives. Rather than trying to fill your newsletter with a random collection of material, you will probably have more success by focusing on a particular subject and relevant calls to action. For example places to visit, future events, tutorials, or interviews with artists and makers. It should be clear on your newsletter subscription page what the nature of the content is and how frequently people can expect to receive them. You could also include links to previous newsletters. Instead of trying to directly sell a product or service, provide engaging content and try to build a relationship with your readers. Marketing messages and calls to action should form a small part of a newsletter and fit naturally within the content, so that readers are more inclined to view them as a beneficial addition, rather than an unwelcome intrusion.

The newsletters that you send might be read on a desktop, tablet or mobile phone and some people could decide to print a hard copy. As part of the proofreading process, you should therefore view newsletters on a range of digital devices. The visual design and writing style should be appropriate for the intended audience and make good use of images to illustrate the text. Encourage subscribers to open newsletters they receive by having attention grabbing subject lines and use descriptive content titles, that encourage people to continue reading. Rather than large blocks of text, write enough to capture the interest of readers, so that they click on a hyperlink, taking them to a landing page on your website, where there is more information. Having online forms that request information about subscriber interests and preferences, could help you to personalise the content. Include within each newsletter, links that enable people to forward them to a friend or share them on social media and provide an unsubscribe link.

The design, delivery and analysis of an email newsletter campaign is a complex process. Look for an email newsletter software platform that will enable you to manage subscriber details, such as name, email address and demographic data. It should also provide suitable templates to ease the design process, including responsive design options. Analytics can be used to monitor statistics, such as open rates and click through rates. You can then compare the performance of different newsletters, looking for ways to make improvements. Using analytics, you could also measure the success rate of conversion funnels and adjust the strategy based on your findings. There are a number of email newsletter services available online and you could read reviews and evaluate some of them, until you find one that is within your budget and suits your requirements. You could decide to use an email marketing service that will also manage the autoresponders in your email marketing campaigns.

Initially you will probably go through a process of testing, including sending different newsletters to sample audience members. You could vary elements such as colour scheme, content layout, font styles, serious or humorous language and use of graphics. The frequency of your newsletters will depend upon your resources, available content and the results from testing and analytics. You could decide to send newsletters every week, month or quarter, but having established the best day and time to deliver them, you should schedule newsletters to be sent on a regular basis. When people are expecting newsletters to arrive on a particular day and at a particular time, they might be more likely to open them. You could allow people to select how often they would like to receive your newsletters and complete online forms describing the type of content that is of greatest interest to them. This could inspire topics for future newsletters, helping you to provide readers with content that they will want to consume and share.

Visual Content

The use of visual content has become an increasingly important part of content marketing and has proven effective in boosting traffic, when used for example within websites and on social media. Visual content such as photographs, illustrations, diagrams, infographics or videos could be used to entertain or inform people in ways that are more engaging than using text alone. This has been confirmed by research which shows that content which includes appropriate visual elements is generally more likely to be understood, remembered and shared. When using visual content, depending upon your skills, resources and available time, you might decide to create it yourself or employ the services of someone else to produce it for you. Alternatively you could decide to pay for stock content or use creative commons content, though you should be aware of any licensing restrictions applying to its use and attribution requirements.

Photographic Content

When using photographs to illustrate their content, many people search online to find stock images, because they assume it is the quickest and most convenient way to locate what they are looking for. However, such images might not be perfectly suited to the message you are trying to convey and an audience could have seen them used elsewhere. Using original photographs has the advantages of their being unique, authentic and appropriate for the message. Owning the copyright will also enable you to prevent photographs being used elsewhere without your permission. If you are producing content to promote your work as an artist or maker, then not only should photographs be original, but the quality of the images will reflect upon the quality of your work. If you lack the necessary skill, then you might decide to hire a professional photographer to get the best results. However, if you regularly create new work and have a large number of items to sell, then you might prefer to take your own photographs. This would mean investing time and money into learning the necessary skills and acquiring the equipment needed to take good product photographs.

When you are going to use photographs in your content marketing, think carefully about where they will be displayed and how they will be perceived. For example, the pictures could feature you working in your studio, creating a piece of work and they could be used on your website to illustrate a blog or tutorial. Photographs could be taken at a craft fair or exhibition, where you are interacting with other people, and each image tagged with relevant information, such as names, date and location. You could ask customers to appear in the photographs with you and record any comments they have about your work. However, when including other people in your photographs, it is polite to request their permission before publishing the pictures online or in print. When potential customers see pictures of your work on a website, within social media or in a printed publication, good quality photographs might increase the chances of an item being purchased.

Digital Photography

Although some professional photographers prefer to use analog film cameras, the vast majority of people taking photographs today use digital cameras. When photographing your work, it is possible to get decent results using a compact camera, though better results could be obtained with a digital SLR. However, if your limited budget means that you will be using the camera on your smartphone, you could still take reasonable pictures. The resolution available with most modern photographic devices is sufficient for images that will be published online. However, if you want to produce high quality framed prints and posters or use the pictures in magazines and physical marketing materials, then you should consider investing in a good camera. The size of the image sensor in a camera determines the amount of light it can collect and the quality of the pictures it can produce. When choosing a photographic device, ensure that it has a macro mode or that you can attach a macro lens, which will enable you to take close up photographs of your work.

Placing items to be photographed within a suitable setting can provide context and scale, whilst using a plain white, coloured or black background focuses attention on the product. Use a tripod to hold your camera steady and get sharply focused pictures. Having arranged a composition, adjust your camera position as required and use a tripod arm to get over head pictures. When taking photographs indoors, placing them within a light box will improve results and using white halogen lights prevents the yellow hue from domestic lighting. If photographs are taken outside during the day, you will benefit from having natural light, whilst shadows can be eliminated using a reflective surface. Understand the ways in which natural light changes between sunrise, midday and sunset, the effect this will have on your photographs and how to adjust camera settings as required. There are various lens filters available that can be used to improve picture quality under different conditions or get particular visual effects. The two most commonly used are UV filters, which can protect the camera lens from environmental damage, and polarising filters, which can improve colour contrast and reduce reflections.

One of the advantages of digital photography is that you can take hundreds or even thousands of pictures and choose the best for use in your content marketing. Photographs could be edited on the digital device used to capture the images or transferred to a computer running photo editing software. You could make improvements to the pictures or apply special effects, although the results that can be achieved will also depend upon the quality of the original image. Carry your camera and accessories in a waterproof protective case or bag, which could also have compartments for spare memory cards, a charger with suitable adapters and a lens and camera cleaning kit. There is a range of paper available onto which you can print images, including photographic quality paper, though you should ensure it is suitable for the inkjet or laser printer that you are using. When purchasing a printer, consider not only the upfront cost, but the cost of consumables such as ink and the output quality. There are also a number of online services, which can supply physical prints of digital photographs or apply images to a wide range of marketing products.

Video Content

Compared with text and static images, video content tends to receive greater levels of engaged traffic. Many popular videos appearing online have been made by amateurs, using software on their home computer to edit footage recorded on a mobile phone or a relatively inexpensive camera. However, if you intend producing a large volume of video content on a regular basis, you might prefer to invest in more professional equipment and learn advanced audio visual skills. The planning and production of a video can be time consuming, requiring an organised schedule, which could include writing a script and using storyboards to visualise each scene within a video. Develop an authentic and engaging presentation style and a content strategy that delivers measurable results. Providing your audience with a greater number of short videos, might attract more traffic than fewer longer videos. If you can afford to do so, then for important projects you might decide to hire the services of an experienced video production team, which should result in audio and video of superior quality.

Video subject matter should be original, entertaining, informative and convey a story worth sharing with your target audience. Whilst developing audio and video production skills, you might already have watched a number of videos and you can now put into practice what you have learned. You could record tutorial videos teaching people artistic techniques, showing people how they can work with particular tools and materials or demonstrating the creation of handmade craft items using specific skills. Topics could also include your working life as an artist or maker, events that you attend, useful lifestyle tips or tutorials demonstrating how damaged items can be repaired. Having produced your videos, you will need some means of delivering them, so that your audience can view them. They could be uploaded, to a social media platform, the most popular of which is YouTube, in addition to being embedded within pages on your website. You might also decide to produce videos for use at events, for example promotional videos about your business and the work that you create.

Content Layout Design

Having devoted time and resources into creating or obtaining original good quality content, you should plan the design of the content layout. For example, when you are using images within a web page, blog post or article they should illustrate what you have written, communicate a message or reinforce a call to action. Also consider whether the layout will be fixed, as with printed publications, or responsive, so that it can adapt to the screen size of the desktop, tablet or mobile telephone it is viewed on. Providing people with information that is organised in a way that is logical and easy to follow, increases the chances that your audience will engage with it in the way that you want them to. Think about how visitors can be guided through content in a way that tells them a story, which engages with them on both an intellectual and emotional level. However, if content elements distract overly from the central message or objective, do not use them just because you think they are pretty or amusing.

Human beings are highly visual and design could be thought of as a language used to communicate with other people through a visual medium, influencing how they think and feel about something. Concepts that you should be aware of when planning your content layout include visual flow, grouping, hierarchy, alignment and focus, along with colour theory. Try to provide an overall experience that is aesthetically pleasing, enhances communication with your audience and eases their decision making. Avoid a cluttered appearance, by using sufficient white space between each element and group related content, highlighting key information. This might for example involve the use of larger or bolded text, borders, boxes, particular fonts and colours. Look at some magazine or website content layouts that you like and ask yourself what about them you think works well. Consider the way in which each element is positioned in relation to the others and how changing them would effect the overall effectiveness of the layout.

Colour theory uses combinations of different colours to produce visual effects and the traditional colour wheel, used by many artists and designers, has twelve colours. The colour wheel consists of the primary colours (red, blue and yellow), secondary colours (green violet and orange) and tertiary colours, which are between the primary and secondary colours. Complementary colours appear on opposite sides of the wheel and can be used to create contrast. Analogous colours are any three that appear alongside each other on the colour wheel. The illusion of perspective can be created by using gradations of colour from light to dark and our perception of colour or size can change when elements of different colour are placed next to each other. Unity refers to the use of related elements to reinforce a theme or purpose and harmony the use of similar shapes and colours. Dominance is the emphasis of more important elements, whilst balance is the positioning of elements that are smaller and larger, or lighter and darker, so that they appear to be of equal visual weight.

CHAPTER 12 ORGANIC AND PAID SEARCH

Search Engines

A search engine is a piece of software, which has been developed for the purpose of locating information available on the internet, such as specific text within websites. Search engines run within browsers and each day millions of people use them, by entering words and phrases related to what they are looking for, such as information on a particular topic or details of a product or service they are considering buying. The results they receive can be either organic or paid and are displayed within a search engine results page (SERP), with each result typically consisting of a title, description and hyperlink to a website landing page. Organic results should match the keywords used to carry out the search and be displayed ranked in order of relevance and quality. Paid for results are displayed when the search terms entered by a user match keywords that an advertiser has included for that particular advert within a campaign. They often appear above organic results, in the form of either text or image adverts.

If you are trying to attract potential customers to your website, then you will want to appear within the SERPs when people search using keywords that relate to your business. Search engine algorithms rank individual web pages rather than entire websites, which can mean that the home page of a website might not appear as highly in the results or receive as much traffic as other pages within a site. Although there are a number of search engines, many businesses focus their resources on trying to find success with Google. However, the strategies employed will also have relevance to other search engines, such as Bing and Yahoo. Secrecy surrounds the details of how search engine algorithms determine the ranking of links to web pages within SERPs.

This reduces the risk of results being manipulated by people who might seek to gain an unfair advantage when trying to attract traffic to their websites.

Search Engine Optimisation

There is much discussion among web professionals regarding the extent to which search engine algorithms use different factors to rank search results. This has led to the growth of Search Engine Optimisation (SEO), which describes the process of trying to improve the position of a web page in organic search results. Those appearing at the top of page one typically attract the most clicks, which can lead to increased traffic and sales for a business. Some people claim to know techniques that will bring quick and easy success. However, each search engine provider is competing to give their users the best and most relevant results for every keyword search that they carry out, therefore by following the search engine providers guidelines you are likely to improve the effectiveness of your SEO. You should therefore focus on having a well designed website, with good page structure and original high quality content, that your target audience is looking for. Ideally SEO will be a consideration throughout the planning, design and development of your website. Although success cannot be guaranteed, having web pages that attract visitors and motivate them to remain on a site, return and backlink, can improve their position within SERPs, in addition to potentially increasing conversion rates.

Keywords and Content

You should have a clear understanding of what your business does and what your customers are looking for. Write down words and phrases related to what you do and which would accurately describe your work and your business to other people. Search online using those terms and make a note of the content appearing at or near the top of search engine results. At the very least you will want to rank highly for your business name and domain name. When putting together your list of keywords, include niche or specialist terms, which although they might be searched for less frequently could bring highly targeted traffic to a website. You could also find that there is less competition for keywords that are being used by fewer people and there is a greater possibility of ranking highly in the SERPs. If you have run paid search campaigns then the results you observed should have enabled you to measure the performance of keywords that you used. What you learned can also inform your choice of keywords to prioritise in organic search.

When you are writing content for your website, using relevant terminology which includes keywords within the text could make web pages more likely to be found by your target audience. Such keywords should form a natural part of writing engaging content and be appropriate for the target audience, so that people reading a page will find information that is relevant to their search terms. People typically search for accurate, up to date information and depending upon the nature of your business you could include regional or seasonal content. Ask family and friends what words and phrases they would use to search online for the products or services that you sell. You could create short questionnaires and ask people who you meet at events to complete them. Consider demographic factors such as gender, age, occupation and hobbies. Ask yourself how content on specific pages might appeal to different people and which keywords could attract them. This could include breaking your content pages down into logical sections or categories, which might make them more likely to be ranked well by search engines and easier for people to navigate.

Meta Tags

Included within the html (hyper text markup language) of web pages, meta tags can be used to provide information about the structure and content of a page. Although not visible when a browser renders the page, meta tags can be seen by viewing the source code. Some meta tags continue to be supported by major search engines and perform a useful function. For example when you search for something online, the description which typically appears within the page of results is an attribute of a meta tag. During the early years of the web, the keywords attribute enabled the authors of web pages to include within meta tags words which they thought best described the page content, influencing the position within organic search results. However, this led to some people using keywords inappropriately and during recent years organisations behind major search engines have stated that keywords within meta tags are no longer an important ranking factor within SERPs.

Among SEO professionals the use of keywords within meta tags continues to be discussed and many recommend that they should either not be used, or if they are then only sparingly. Concerns raised include the risk that the misuse of keywords might cause web pages to be penalised in the SERPs. Also keywords within meta tags can be viewed in the source code of a web page, revealing them to competitors. Instead your time would be better spent writing good quality original content that engages with readers and includes suitable page titles and descriptions. Keywords used within the text that is visible on a web page, continue to be a factor in how a page will be ranked in SERPs. However, they should occur naturally and the overuse of keywords and phrases could have a negative impact on both user experience and page performance.

Website Design

Although a search engine is not able to appreciate the aesthetics of a website in the way that a human being can, there are elements of site design that can assist both a human visitor and the algorithm indexing a web page. Try to have a purpose for each page, for example a product page, blog post or article and give the web page a name that describes the content. Having a short descriptive SEO friendly web address or URL (Uniform Resource Locator) for each page could help to improve their ranking in search engines. It could also be easier for people to remember the URL and make it more likely pages might be bookmarked or shared. Although the title tag text is not displayed in the body of a web page, it should accurately describe the content of a web page, as it is the text that appears as a hyperlink in SERPs which people click on to open a page. The title tag text also appears in the title bar when a page is viewed in a browser and as the default text when a page is bookmarked.

Search engine algorithms are attempting to determine how good a web page will be for a human visitor. Therefore you should focus on creating web pages for people. Within the body of a web page, heading titles should accurately describe the text above which they appear and indicate the prioritisation of information provided. When words within a sentence appear in bold this will indicate that they are of greater importance. High quality images can enhance the look of a website, but you should also provide descriptive image names and alt tags, which can improve accessibility for screen readers. When creating content for your website consider communications that you might also have with people offline, such as at arts and crafts events. Try to establish good integration between your online and real world marketing and branding. The use of Cascading Style Sheets (CSS) enables content and design to be separated, helping to improve page performance, ease site management and increase responsiveness when viewed on different mobile and desktop devices.

Personas

When you are searching for keywords and planning the structure and content of a website, it can help to envisage the journeys that people might take when finding and using the site. The creation of fictional individuals, called personas can assist in this process. The personas could be based upon people that you know, answers to marketing questionnaires or customer interviews. Include information that could influence decision making, such as demographic data, their interests and how they consume different products and services. Though fictional, personas can help to make an audience seem more real, focusing attention upon end user needs and benefits, rather than assuming people will behave in the same way that you would. If there are a number of people working on a website, the use of personas can help everyone to have a clearer understanding of the target audience that the site needs to attract and engage with. This can inform decisions regarding the visual design, development, content and marketing of a website.

Backlinks

A backlink is a hyperlink in a web page that leads visitors to another web page that is located within a different website. The value of a backlink to your website depends upon factors such as its relevance and the quality of the page linking to your site. When a web page has many high quality relevant backlinks pointing to it, this can be an indicator of quality. In addition to directly attracting visitors, this could also contribute towards improved ranking in search engine results. To attract backlinks from people who are genuinely interested in your content and want to share it with other people, create good quality original content, such as articles or a blog based upon your experiences as an artist or maker. Only add a backlink leading to another website if you genuinely want to share content that someone else has included within that page, not as a result of taking part in some type of link exchange, as this could risk damaging the reputation of your website.

Build relationships online with other people who share your interests, by for example commenting on blog posts and joining in forum discussions on relevant topics. You could also create pages that people are more likely to want to backlink, by including within them content such as articles, infographics, videos and tutorials. Being active on social media platforms that are popular with your target audience could help to raise awareness of your website. A good PR campaign could also lead to coverage in high profile online or print publications. When you engage effectively with other people, they will be more likely to read what you have written. They might also add backlinks within their web pages and like or follow you on social media. If people that you develop relationships with online are influential and have many followers, their backlinks could bring increasing numbers of visitors to your website who are genuinely in interested in what you do.

Paid Search

During recent years advertising budgets have increasingly moved online and away from traditional forms of advertising, within media such as newspapers, radio and television. Much of that money has been spent on paid search, in the form of Pay Per Click (PPC). Among the benefits of PPC compared to print or broadcast media, is that it can be more accurately targeted and measured. Whilst you pay the same for traditional advertising regardless of how many people see or respond to it, with PPC you only pay when an online advertising link is clicked on, so that someone can visit the web page to which it is linked. Therefore whilst many people might see an online advert, resulting in a large number of impressions, you only pay when they decide to click on the hyperlink. You can then measure how many of those visitors go on to complete actions that you want them to carry out, such as purchasing a product or service.

PPC adverts will generally appear among other ads that have been created by competing advertisers and the quality of an advert can influence whether someone will click on it. The purpose of an advert is to attract the attention of your target audience, so that when they visit the web page to which it is linked they will find content that they are searching for. It is therefore important that the keywords you include with each advert are relevant to the search terms people are likely to use. The position of an advert in SERPs is influenced by factors such as the amount bid for keywords and the quality score, determined by the relevance and quality of an advert and the web page to which it is linked. Consequently a good quality website landing page with relevant content can benefit from having paid adverts that rank more highly and cost the advertiser less than another advertiser with a poorer quality landing page. This helps to ensure that people find content that is relevant to the terms they enter into a search engine.

A typical PPC advert consists of clickable headline text, a display URL and a description. PPC campaigns contain adverts that can be organised into related ad groups and appear within a search engine results page, when keywords and phrases are searched for, or on a website that is part of a display network. When creating a PPC campaign think about words that people might type into a search engine when looking for information about the products or services that you sell. The keywords should also be relevant to the landing page to which you are directing traffic. You could research related terms that people might use, comparing the volume of potential targeted traffic. For example if you were selling kits for making greeting cards, then an ad group including the term card making kits could attract via PPC visitors who want to make their own greeting cards. The advert could be linked to a landing page on your website which has a guide to making your own greeting cards and people arriving on that page could decide to purchase one or more of your card making kits.

The PPC adverts that you start will run between the dates and times you have specified, or until the amount spent reaches the daily budget that you have set. After running the adverts for some time, review the performance of each. Based upon the results you might decide to increase or decrease the future budget for a particular campaign or ad group. Using the average cost per click and the conversion rate percentage, you can calculate the cost per conversion. If any ads are costing you more money than their value to you through initial and future sales, you could decide to stop them running, whilst increasing the budget for those that are profitable. You should exclude from adverts words or phrases attracting search traffic that does not convert well. For example the term greeting cards is likely to attract people who want to buy cards, but might be less interested in buying card making kits, which would be a waste of your PPC budget. You could also exclude words such as cheap or free, which might result in you paying for ad clicks that are less likely to convert into a sale.

Rather than being a one off activity that you complete and then forget about, developing a PPC campaign should be an ongoing process. With each advert that you create, go through a repeated cycle of finding suitable keywords, running adverts, measuring their performance and then making improvements. Your objective should be to run a profitable PPC campaign, which will bring to your website relevant high quality traffic, that converts into new customers and increased sales. Some adverts could be seasonal and others designed to promote a specific product, service or event. There are tools available such as the Google Adwords Keyword Planner, which enables you to compare search volumes and bid prices for related keywords, looking for both positive and negative terms. Whilst some businesses choose to outsource the management of their PPC campaign, you are the expert at what your business does and best placed to know what your customers are looking for. If you choose to hire someone else to manage your PPC campaign, spend some time with them to ensure they understand the type of visitors that you want to attract to your website.

Analytics

Software such as Google Analytics, enables you to monitor metrics relating to website usage. The data is anonymised, but provides a wide range of useful information such as the volume of visitors landing on each page, geographical data, demographic information and the device types people are using. Data can be viewed on a timeline so that you can compare performance over days, weeks, months and years. When you are running PPC or marketing campaigns, you will be able to monitor how effectively they are performing and how well different pages are converting visitors into engaged users and customers. Based upon your findings you could then make changes to your site or campaigns and observe the results.

Digital Marketing Agencies

Although you could learn the skills needed to manage your own organic and paid search campaigns, you might at some point decide to employ the services of a digital marketing agency. When choosing an agency you could begin by seeking recommendations from other people or searching online. Look for an agency that takes the time to develop a good working relationship with each client, so that they understand their business and its needs. Researching agencies online could help you to gauge how effective their marketing services appear to have been for their existing and possibly former clients. Be wary of any agency that promises to deliver unrealistic results or doesn't seem to have a clear understanding of what is involved in running a successful marketing campaign. An agency should be able to give you top of the funnel (TOFU) traffic numbers, based upon their previous experience of running similar campaigns. However, they will not be able to tell you how many sales to expect from a campaign, until they know how well your business is able to convert any resulting leads that you receive into sales.

A digital marketing agency could offer their clients a range of services. They might include; researching keywords for use across websites, social media and newsletters, applying SEO principles to improve organic search results, managing PPC campaigns, reducing landing page bounce rates and increasing Conversion Rate Optimisation (CRO). Agencies could create customer personas, considering how each visitor type might navigate a website, to ensure they find relevant content, regardless of which page within the site they first land on. Other tasks they could undertake include reviewing website structure, developing more effective content marketing strategies and improving page layout. Such efforts could increase the time visitors spend on each page, the number of other pages they visit within a site and encourage them to return. Digital marketing agencies could work to increase brand awareness and customer engagement, by helping you to make more effective use of social media, running PR campaigns and attracting good quality backlinks from influencers. They could design personalised email newsletters, set up permission based email marketing campaigns and run online surveys. Agencies could also develop strategies to integrate digital marketing campaigns with more traditional broadcast and print media.

When comparing quotes by agencies and prices listed on their website or rate card, think in terms of the value to your business of the services they are offering. Your marketing budget will probably be determined by factors such as current revenue and profits, forecast growth and expected future returns. The main ways that an agency provides value is by reducing costs or increasing revenue and profits. You should know the average lifetime value (LTV) and cost of customer acquisition (COCA) for your business. Using these values it will then be possible to determine how effective a marketing campaign has been, after it has been running long enough for a strategy to produce measurable results. By understanding and explaining the analytics data, a marketing agency should be able to demonstrate how effective their work has been with regards to objectives such as increased targeted website traffic, new customer sales and existing customer retention. You can then discuss the results with the agency and decide whether it is worth continuing with the marketing campaign, if the campaign needs to be changed in some way or if you would prefer to find a different agency to manage your marketing.

CHAPTER 13 SOCIAL MEDIA

Social Media Strategy

Each day millions of people visit social media platforms to consume, post and share messages and content. An effective social media strategy could help you to reach some of those people, raising your profile as an artist, designer or craft maker. You could find new customers for your work and build an ongoing relationship with them. When planning your strategy, in addition to understanding how to use the different platforms, it can be helpful to consider why social media is so popular and some of the psychology involved in its use. For example words such as find, follow, like, join or share, can prompt action and when we experience positive feedback our brain releases feel good chemicals. Many people enjoy learning new things or feeling part of a select group that has access to exclusive content. Some might want to be the first to share a new piece of content or information with other people, perhaps because they hope to impress them. When posting content, you could try appealing to your followers natural curiosity about other people and the world around them.

Traditional media such as television, radio and print publishing can provide a platform for broadcasting messages to an audience. However, reaching people through social media requires a different approach. They are looking for a more meaningful conversation and often share how they think and feel about themselves, each other and a subject, product or service that is of interest to them. Rather than measuring social media success only in terms of the number of likes, followers or subscribers, the level of engagement is increasingly important. When a business builds a community around what they do, by providing relevant content and motivating user engagement, they are more likely to inspire brand loyalty. Rather than customers being passive consumers of a product or service, they can become supportive and actively promote brands that they like. Listening to and understanding the audience that they are trying to reach, can enable a business to appeal to customers more directly. As an artist or maker you are in an excellent position to do this, without the need for a large marketing budget, by sharing with other people your passion for creating handmade work.

Although social media has become increasingly popular, most human communication still takes place in the real world. Therefore you should look for ways in which what you post online can connect your business to the real world in which people live and work. For example including references to an object or experience that people might find in their daily life, could prompt a potential customer into remembering your social media post, your brand and the products or services that you sell. We have many choices when it comes to how we spend our free time and you should consider how you might be able to provide the sort of content that people are looking for. People like to consume and share content that entertains them, such as funny or inspiring stories, or provides useful information and this could attract increasing numbers of followers. Sharing what we care about also makes us feel better about ourselves and can reinforce or improve the impression that we want other people to have of us.

Thought Leaders

Throughout human history and across cultures, like minded people have come together to build communities and achieve common goals. Often they were led by a political, military or spiritual leader who convinced people that they could achieve more by working together than would be possible on their own. Leaders who were able to attract such a following did so by inspiring others with a clear message and purpose. This motivated people towards achieving a common goal by working together to overcome obstacles standing in their path. Although such behaviour might seem out of place in relation to attracting a following online, most people still want to feel part of a community and will look for like minded people who share their interests. Rather than being limited to individuals they meet in real life, people can now use social media to communicate with each other all over the world. They can engage on a more personal level with individuals or organisations than is possible through broadcast media. However, when planning a social media strategy, a business will need to consider the time and resources needed to manage online engagement.

The term thought leader has been applied to individuals or organisations whose words and deeds inspire others to follow them. They might have had great success in fields such as politics, science, business, sport or the arts. Thought leaders are often admired and trusted, becoming role models. They might decide to share insights into their work or private life through broadcast or social media. This provides an opportunity for such thought leaders to share with their followers the path that they are following. Rather than relying solely upon facts and figures, social influencers and leaders can affect how people think, feel and behave by recognising their hopes and fears and inspiring them with a vision that understands their aspirations. People could attend events where they are able to hear and meet thought leaders that inspire them. Followers coming together in such a way might find a sense of community. This could reinforce feelings of loyalty and strengthen their belief that the path they are following is shaping their life in a positive way.

Using social media, it is possible to reach many people, with a clear strong message or brand identity and stand out in crowded market. For example if you have an interest or passion, such as your work as an artist or maker, then you could share what you do with the aim of attracting a following online. You could post pictures of your work, talk about what inspires you and express thoughts and feelings about what you do and why. If you have considerable skill and experience in an art or craft, then you could answer questions from people who want to learn and need advice. You might begin to be considered an expert or thought leader and you could encourage like minded people to join in the conversation with you and other followers. People could be motivated to share what you say with their family and friends, both online and in real life. Over time you could establish a network of people sharing their ideas and experiences with yourself and each other.

In popular culture there are many examples of celebrities, artists and fashionable brands that have become thought leaders and attract a loyal following. They do so by appealing to our human need to join together with other people and feel like we belong to a group with shared values. We also like to feel that we are special in some way that differentiates us and our group from other people and the groups to which they belong. People can be drawn to individuals or organisations who appeal to them on an intellectual or emotional level, by seeming to understand what they want and need. It can be difficult forming genuine relationships based upon shared values, interests and mutual respect and many people are searching for greater meaning and purpose in their life and work. Social media provides an opportunity to bring people together to exchange thoughts, feelings and experiences with people they might not otherwise meet. As they engage more deeply around their shared interests, people can develop a sense of community values and loyalty to each other.

Marketing professionals are often employed by large organisations to develop strategies that are designed to promote a product or service to a target audience. This includes creating messages that appeal to our subconscious mind, which influences much of our decision making. For example an organisation could publish research results that highlight the benefits of something that they supply, as part of a campaign to promote themselves to their target audience. However, as an artist or craft maker you are in a position to build relationships with your followers that are based upon genuine engagement and shared interests. When you join social media platforms, follow other people who you find to be informative and inspirational. Manage messages, comments and mentions that you find online about yourself or your business in a friendly professional manner, responding to or acknowledging them as appropriate. By investing time and energy into your social media presence in an effective way, you could attract increasing numbers of engaged followers, leading to new creative opportunities and raising the profile of your work with potential customers.

Attracting a Following

According to the theory of six degrees of separation each person in the world is within six steps of everyone else, through their various social interactions. Although this has been disputed, due for example to the existence of remote isolated populations, it is possible to attract a large following by sharing content on social media. Many people dream of having a viral hit that spreads rapidly across the world, reaching a huge audience and attracting many followers. However, there are millions of videos and billions of messages and photographs shared online each day, of which only a tiny proportion become viral and simply copying what has worked for others is unlikely to lead to success. Focus instead upon creating messages and content that will appeal to your target audience, rather than worrying about creating the next Internet sensation. For example a catchy tune in an amusing video or a relatable quote in a piece of text might remind people of your business brand and your work. This could help to raise awareness online, attract more followers and enable you to engage with potential customers.

When deciding what stories to share online about your work as an artist or craft maker, recall people or places that have inspired you. Think about the learning process that you had to go through to be able to create your work and the years of experience involved in reaching your current level of skill. Reflect upon your USP, mission statement and vision statements. Consider how you could incorporate ideas that relate to your business within the narrative of a story or a piece of content, so as to engage with your audience and motivate sharing. Videos of seemingly mundane tasks can be popular online, such as unboxing and reviewing items that someone has purchased.

Most of us will remember the excitement and expectation of unwrapping a gift, wondering what it might be and enjoying the element of surprise. In addition to curiosity, there is the practical benefit of learning about a product which the viewer might be considering purchasing. Tutorials teaching practical skills are popular, as are useful tips, such as how to restore damaged furniture or textiles.

Most of us prefer spending time with people whose company we enjoy and are more likely to follow someone on social media who we relate to and admire. This has led to many celebrities having huge followings online and being able influence their followers. Companies that are keen for their products and services to be endorsed by such celebrities might give limited edition or exclusive fashion items to people who have a lifestyle that their followers aspire to. This could give the celebrity a feeling that they are valued, respected or belong to a cultural elite and they might share messages on social media that promote those brands. However, social influencers who attract many followers can also be trusted peers rather than celebrities and although you might not reach their level of success, you could still attract growing numbers of followers who appreciate the quality of your work. They might decide to share your posts with their own followers, helping you to reach a wider audience.

Social Media and Email

Social media can raise awareness of a brand and open communication with an audience, however you might have less control than when people engage with you on your own website or subscribe to your email list. Research has shown that email can be more effective than social media when it comes to motivating customers to purchase a product or service. Therefore social media should not be used in isolation, but coordinated with other marketing and communication activities. When you engage with people through social media, asking them to opt in to receiving emails will enable you to build an email list and begin sending direct personalised messages. You could offer those people who leave their email address a free newsletter or access to a free tutorial. Understanding your audience should enable you to create messages that support a relationship of trust, respecting what people think and how they feel. Learn from individuals and businesses that have made effective use of social media and email. For example you could email highly engaged followers on social media to thank them for their support and offer to send them free samples of your work.

Comparing Social Media Platforms

The use of social media has grown rapidly during recent years and when planning your social media strategy it is worthwhile trying to understand the characteristics of each platform. You could join and compare a number of them, before deciding which to focus your efforts on. Consider the ways in which your target audience uses social media and how you can engage with them. When searching for news and opinions, or communicating with family, friends and organisations, people might visit their preferred social media site to share their thoughts and feelings. People tend to use Facebook to communicate with their existing contacts and post content that is intended to have some longevity, providing an opportunity to increase engagement. By contrast Twitter posts are typically short, being limited initially to 140 characters, though during 2017 the limit was increased to 280 characters. They tend to be ephemeral and intended for consumption by people who are more likely to be strangers. If you want to begin engaging with new people who are in your target audience, then you are more likely to find them by using Google Plus or Twitter, where you can follow people that you do not know.

Effective engagement with an audience on social media will require you to commit time and resources. Therefore you might get better results by focusing on just one or two platforms that give you the best return on investment (ROI), rather than spreading your efforts too thin across many of them. Your social media biography or profile should represent your brand, whether you join as a business or under your own name, perhaps as an artist or maker. Although different platforms are competing with each other for users, they tend to have features that make each of them better suited to a certain form or style of communication and might be popular with a particular demographic group. Users of particular platforms could be interested in content that you are sharing and more likely to engage with you. Specific social media platforms might therefore prove more effective than others as a means of attracting new customers. Some sites also encourage the use of paid advertising to promote business brands and messages.

Monitor social media sites and respond to any comments about your business, investigating complaints and thanking people for positive feedback. Search for people who you would like to follow and engage with, contributing relevant posts to conversations. They might be fellow artists and makers, part of your target audience or experts and social influencers who you can learn from. Along with posting your own comments and content that you think will be of interest to your followers, share informative, inspiring or amusing posts made by other people who you are following. They might share your content with their followers and this could help to raise your social profile, rather than your presence being perceived as just a sales vehicle. Including suitable photographs and videos with your posts can also help to make them stand out. In addition to Facebook, Google Plus and Twitter, there are many other popular social networking websites, including YouTube, LinkedIn, Instagram and Pinterest. However, in the rapidly changing world of social media whilst some platforms attract many users and thrive, others fail to take off or decline in popularity and marketing reach.

Facebook

Facebook is widely used to share messages and content with family and friends, such as personal photographs and videos, or organise social events. Rather than a personal page, businesses can use a business page and including relevant links within web pages, email signatures and marketing material could help customers find you on Facebook. Understand who you are trying to engage with and why, creating a profile with text and images that reflect your business brand, but consider that users will probably be in the mood to relax, socialise or play games. Rather than trying to broadcast marketing or sales messages, Facebook provides an opportunity to build relationships with customers through deeper engagement and sharing interesting content that will appeal to them. For example you could post stories about your creative journey as an artist or craft maker, encouraging other people to share their stories with you.

Twitter

Many people use Twitter to follow celebrities, comment on products and services or share updates from live events. Although images can be included with tweets, it is a primarily text based medium and the limited character length lends itself to posting quick messages. Individuals and organisations tend to tweet more frequently than they post Facebook updates and tweets can be scheduled to go out on particular dates and at specific times of the day. Regularly posting original interesting messages could encourage people to follow you and including suitable hashtags can help people to find what you post. Consider how the design of your Twitter page and each message sent reflects upon your business brand. Messages could include amusing or inspiring thoughts for the day. Posts without hyperlinks to external content might attract greater engagement and only including links in posts to relevant content when appropriate, can help them stand out. Analytics could be used to measure and compare the effectiveness of different tweets, regarding their content and when they were sent.

Google Plus

Users of Google Plus tend to be more interested in finding information and discussing a subject of interest to them, rather than socialising. Start by adding people that you know and then search for subjects that are of interest to you, such as an art or craft that you practice. When you begin to follow someone, you will be able to see their publicly published posts. You can organise people who you follow by adding them to circles, such as Family, Friends or Acquaintances. This will enable you to filter the content that you share with each group and you can create your own circles, suitable for business or social communication. When you post content, it can either be public or private, for example only visible to members of a particular circle. However, what you post will only appear automatically in the stream of other users if they have chosen to follow you. You could engage with other people by joining discussions on topics of interest to you or begin new discussions and share content which might attract followers.

YouTube

Each day millions of people around the world watch videos on YouTube, which can be searched for within the YouTube site and appear in search engine results. Videos can vary in length from less than a minute to several hours. Those creating and uploading videos to their channel might be professional or amateur film makers, businesses promoting products and services or people sharing videos with family, friends or the wider public. After you login to your Google account, you will be able to create your own YouTube channel. When customising your channel, you should try to reflect your business brand, by for example using an appropriate channel name, well designed channel art and a suitable channel description. Help people to find videos that you upload, by including descriptive titles, good descriptions and relevant keywords. In addition to being a video sharing platform, YouTube is a social networking site and by allowing people who subscribe to your channel to comment on your videos you could open up a dialogue with them. You could encourage communication by asking relevant questions.

Rather than a small number of long videos, successful channels on YouTube tend to host many videos, though they might each only have a running time of a few minutes. Uploading new videos on a regular basis, perhaps the same day each week, could attract a growing number of viewers. The videos could be one off productions or form a series on related topics, organised into playlists. Rather than worrying about being the next viral hit, deliver content that will inform, entertain and tell a story that you want to share with your target audience. Learn how to build a successful channel, by attracting subscribers and use analytics to measure visitor traffic and engagement. Encourage people to subscribe to your channel and share videos that they like with family and friends. You could contact other people who are also running YouTube channels that attract a similar audience to your own and suggest some cross promotion, which could attract new viewers. A well managed YouTube channel attracting a large number of subscribers could form an effective part of your content marketing strategy.

LinkedIn

LinkedIn was designed for professional and business users as a platform on which people can highlight their job history and experience, connecting with other professionals. The business to business nature of LinkedIn makes it a useful service for those wanting to recruit personnel, strengthen their brand or establish credentials as a thought leader among their peers. You could enhance your profile on LinkedIn by adding content such as presentations and videos. People can create or join groups related to their area of expertise and meet others working in the same field. Within such groups users could post or answer questions and potentially develop business relationships, although there might be less frequent engagement between users of LinkedIn than some other social media platforms. Rather than just posting self-promoting sales pitches, take the time to read the profiles of other people, before trying to establish genuine mutually beneficial communications. When starting or joining discussions on a particular topic, become someone who provides advice and support that other people trust and respect. Over time you could become part of a network of engaged professionals, which could lead to new business opportunities.

Pinterest

Individuals and organisations using Pinterest to promote their brand and attract customers, can post images, called pins, that are linked to external content. Pinterest is highly visual and you should ensure that the pictures you post stand out and capture the attention of viewers, by being high quality and depicting interesting subject matter. The images can be organised into categories using boards, for example different types of art or handmade crafts that you create or workshops that you run teaching creative skills. Understand what your target audience will be searching for and include relevant keywords within the descriptive text for each image, to help people find them. Regularly add new images to attract followers, who you could then communicate with directly. People clicking on an image that you have uploaded could be taken to a website landing page, containing relevant and engaging content. Use analytics to monitor how well each image that you post is performing, so that you can add more images of the type that are attracting the most clicks and conversions.

Instagram

Instagram was launched in the year 2010 as a mobile app and enables users to share videos, photographs and updates of where they are and what they doing. Posts can be either public or private, so that they will only be seen by approved followers. Individuals and organisations can use the service to market their personal or business brand and the visual nature of Instagram allows artists and makers to showcase their work. Including suitable keywords within descriptions and hashtags can help people to find relevant content. The use of good quality images and videos, with interesting subject matter, can help posts stand out, attracting followers and encouraging engagement. Rather than posting a generic sales pitch, take the time to understand what will appeal to your target audience and develop a strategy with clearly defined and measurable objectives. Create inspiring stories around your brand, that can be told using visual content and post regularly. Within your account biography, link to relevant content, such as your blog or a landing page on your website. Analyse the performance of your posts, to improve your strategy and get better results.

CHAPTER 14 COURSES AND WORKSHOPS

Aptitude and Skills

When you are considering starting a business, it is sensible to base it upon something in which you have an active interest and some aptitude or experience. There are a wide range of arts and crafts disciplines that have the potential to provide an income and upon which a business could be founded. You might want to make a hobby into a full time business, with the aim of becoming a successful artist or craft maker. If you already possess the necessary skills and experience, then you might only need to obtain the required tools and materials or find a suitable place to work. However, you could decide that you need to learn new skills or improve upon existing skills.

You could begin learning the basic principles of an art or craft by reading books or how to guides and watching tutorial videos online. However, you are likely to make greater progress in the acquisition of practical skills if you attend an appropriate course or workshop, where you can observe other people practicing their art or craft. Studying and working alongside experienced artists and makers could allow you to compare the quality of your work with theirs, boost your confidence and provide an opportunity for you to meet other creative people. They might give you valuable advice, sharing some of what they have learned over the years.

Formal Education and Training

An art or craft is learned over many years of study and practice, which includes working alongside people who have already mastered the relevant skills and techniques. For centuries, traditional skills were passed from generation to generation through apprenticeships, which would typically last for a number of years. The apprentice would enter into a legal contract with a company or master, who through instruction and example would teach them about the tools, materials and techniques used in their work. They would learn how to correctly select tools, choose materials and evaluate the quality of the work that they were able to produce. Following an apprenticeship, the individual would work for a number of years as a journeyman, until their work reached a required standard and they earned recognition as a master craftsman in their own right. As they progressed and began developing an intuitive feel for the tools and materials that they worked with, they were able to create work of superior quality.

The Industrial Revolution led to the decline of many traditional skills, as mass production meant that workers were increasingly employed in large factories doing repetitive work. Although apprenticeships still existed, technical schools and colleges emerged, providing vocational education to complement on the job training. In the United Kingdom the City and Guilds of London Institute, founded in 1878, awards vocational qualifications in areas such as engineering, construction, health care, business, design, arts and crafts. Those wishing to demonstrate superior skill in a particular craft can still acquire the title of Master Craftsman. In the United States trade schools opened during the nineteenth and twentieth century, providing vocational and technical education to complement on the job training, in order to provide the skilled workforce needed by the nations rapidly growing industries. Many art, craft and design disciplines can be studied on short college courses or to degree, masters degree or PhD level.

Attending a Course or Workshop

You might not have sufficient time or resources to commit to years of formal education and training in a particular art or craft. Indeed whilst going through such a process can contribute to the formation of creative talent, some people have achieved success through self-directed learning. However, many people find that attending a suitable course or workshop is a worthwhile exercise. You should look for one that is run by people who already posses the skills that you want to learn, along with a good level of practical experience. Also remember that some people are experts in their field, but lack the ability to teach, whilst others are able to communicate effectively with their students, inspiring them to learn deeply and tap into their own creative potential.

When looking for a course or workshop, you could search online for those being held in your area and contact local colleges, to enquire about classes they are running. You could also seek advice from exhibitors that you meet at events, people you communicate with online or family and friends. The teaching should be at a level which is appropriate for your current ability. For example, if you are a novice, then you might struggle in a class designed for more advanced students. By contrast you could be wasting your time and money attending a class which is too easy for you and doesn't provide you with an opportunity to improve your skills and learn new techniques.

Before investing time and money in a new business, you should ensure that you have the necessary aptitude and skills. Setting up the business might involve purchasing expensive tools, equipment and materials. Depending on the nature of what you will be doing and the availability of suitable work space within your home, you might also need to rent a studio or workshop. If you are uncertain which art or craft you want to build your business upon, then you could try a few different disciplines before making a decision. Attending a course which will provide you with the relevant tools, materials and working environment, would give you an opportunity to see if it is a good fit for you. You could also join some local artists and makers groups. Practice creating things to sell at local events, until you feel confident enough to commit to going into business full time.

Running a Course or Workshop

If you have developed a high level of skill in your chosen art or craft, along with considerable experience, then you might decide to earn an additional income by running your own courses or workshops. Teaching other people how to create hand made items, could complement the business of selling your own work. Students might want to improve their hobby skills, learn how to make personalised gifts for family and friends or have ambitions to sell what they make. Teaching classes could also help to raise your profile and enhance your reputation as an artist or maker. For example you could create online tutorials and engage with other people through social media. This might help to increase sales of your work and attract more commissions. You could also package and sell craft kits, containing tools, materials and instructions, with which people would be able to make craft items on their own.

Some artists and makers might worry that their students could copy their style and that they might consequently lose sales to them in the future. This is something that you must decide for yourself. However, if you have developed a recognisable style over a number of years, which reflects your unique creative vision, this might be less of a concern. You could encourage the students you teach to invest the time and energy required to apply what they have learned to develop their own distinct style. Rather than lacking the confidence to make something original, they might choose themes or subject matter that appeal to them and inspire their creativity. After much study and practice, your students could develop their own creative talents and begin creating unique handmade work of their own.

In addition to understanding the subject that you want to teach, you will also need to posses good communication skills and the ability to convey effectively the content of your lessons to each student. If you have previously taught or trained other people, even if it was in an unrelated field, then you might already possess the appropriate skills. However, if you lack such experience and are unsure whether you have an aptitude for teaching other people, then you could decide to learn the necessary skills. You could read books, watch videos or attend courses on the planning and delivery of educational material. Before investing time and resources into your new venture, run a few practice sessions with family and friends, to see if this is something that you will want to do long term. These people could also provide you with useful feedback regarding your performance.

Finding Students and Taking Bookings

People interested in attending a course or workshop might have approached you previously and if you kept a record of their contact details you could invite them. Raise awareness of what you will be teaching, where and when among your network of contacts, including family and friends. Print leaflets which can be distributed at events where you are exhibiting your work. Create a page on your website, where people can learn about any courses or workshops that you will be running. Also promote them through social media or relevant groups of which you are a member and advertise online or within print publications that are read by your target audience. Be clear whether classes will be appropriate for novice or more advanced students, along with the tools and materials that you will be providing for use on the day. Suitable online questionnaires could guide people towards the course or workshop that will be best suited to their current level of skill and experience. Describe the venue where you will be teaching and estimate the number of students expected to attend.

Clearly state the cost of booking a place, provide convenient methods of payment and include details of any relevant terms and conditions that apply. To avoid any awkwardness, rather than accepting payment by cash on the day, you might prefer to request and receive payment from each student, before confirming their place on the course or workshop. Booking forms could be based upon suitable templates, helping you to provide a consistent level of service. Having confirmed the date, time and venue with each student that will be attending, send an email containing information that they will need to be aware of, so that they arrive properly prepared on the day. This should include transport links, directions and areas they can safely park. Details could also be placed within a section of your website that is only accessible to yourself and the students who have confirmed places. Send a reminder to each student as the date that they have booked to attend approaches. If for any reason you need to cancel a course or workshop, then you should inform people promptly and politely, offering alternative dates or a full refund.

Course or Workshop Venue

When you decide to teach a course or workshop, one of the first things that you must do is find an appropriate venue. Holding them within your own home would remove the cost of hiring a venue, but there could be other costs, such as converting a room into a teaching space. This would require equipment and resources, including seating, lighting, work surfaces and possibly access to sinks and power points. There would need to be sufficient storage for tools and materials and enough room for your students to work, while allowing you to move easily and safely among them to monitor their progress. The teaching environment that you create should be relaxed and conducive to learning, without distractions such as other family members or pets. However, the room in which classes are held could also serve as a studio, in which to create and display your own work. Discuss your plans with anyone else that you share your home with and consider how setting up a dedicated space within your home might affect family life.

Make it clear where students are allowed to take photographs, which they might want to share with family and friends and on social media. If you do not have a dedicated entry way and students will be walking through shared areas of your home, then you could request that they remove their shoes or provide them with non-slip shoe covers. To reduce the risk of any awkward or embarrassing situations, clearly signpost rooms that students are allowed to enter and those that are private, for example a second toilet could be made available for their use. Remove personal property from the room or place it in locked cupboards, rather than risk it being lost or damaged. To prevent coats and bags cluttering the teaching area, you should provide a cloak room and suggest that people keep valuables such as wallets and purses on their person. You could also recommend people clearly label their belongings, to avoid any confusion that could arise if people bring similar looking coats, laptops or bags.

Rather than running a course or workshop from within your own home, you might decide to hire a venue. You could search online for somewhere suitable and seek advice from your network of contacts. Having drawn up a shortlist of those that are within your budget, you could visit each of them and book the venue which best meets your requirements. Consider factors such as the travel distance from home, the quality of the facilities and accessibility of the location for yourself and potential students. Possible benefits of hiring a purpose built teaching environment, could include having sufficient space and resources on site to hold larger classes and generate more income. Good transport links should allow people to travel more easily to the venue and there could be greater availability of parking spaces for their vehicles. However, you would probably have to set up each class before running it and clear away again afterwards and take account of the time and cost involved in transporting yourself and any tools or materials each way.

Class Size and Pricing

You need to know how many students you can effectively and safely teach within the proposed venue. Depending upon the nature of what you will be teaching, a class size of between six and ten could be considered reasonable. Having too few students might mean that you struggle to become economically viable. However, trying to teach too many students could reduce the time and attention available for each of them to the point where they do not learn effectively and you fail to deliver value for money. You could base your decision upon the experience of attending a course or workshop as a student. There could also be greater flexibility regarding student numbers when hiring a purpose built venue rather than using a room within your own home.

The amount that you decide to charge each student will depend upon your overall running costs and the profit that you want to earn. Some costs will be incurred on a per student basis when classes are run, such as materials used and refreshments consumed, if you supply them. Other up front costs could be returned over a number of months or years. For example you should add to each booking fee a small amount to cover the purchase of tools and equipment, along with adapting a suitable room, if you are holding classes within your own home. Also include the cost of any wages, marketing, advertising and insurance and remember to set aside money that you will be required to pay in taxes.

Equipment and Supplies

Having determined what you will be teaching and to how many students, you should ensure that you have the necessary resources. Be clear before people book a place on your course or workshop, whether you will be providing all of the tools, materials and equipment that they will need to complete the set projects. If students will be expected to bring anything with them, then they should be made aware of this and it should be reflected in the price that you charge. Always have a sufficient stock of materials and keep tools in good working order, including spares to replace any that cannot be used due to damage or loss. Students should not be forced to waste time waiting to use shared tools. You should also have a good supply of sundry items that people might need such as pens and paper, as well as cleaning materials, a first aid kit and safety equipment such as fire extinguishers.

Food and Drink

After working for a couple of hours, people might begin to get tired and lose their concentration, therefore you should split the day up into manageable sections. If you are intending the course or workshop that you teach to run for a full working day, then you should consider provision of suitable refreshments and allow time for morning and afternoon breaks and lunch. You could provide a comfortable seated area where people can eat and drink and which is away from the working space. This will prevent spilled drinks damaging equipment or materials and allow the students to relax and chat, also enabling them to network with other attendees. If the weather is pleasant, then providing access to a garden or other suitable outside area would allow people to enjoy some fresh air.

To ensure that your students do not need to go out and look for a place where they can buy food and drink, you should either recommend they bring a packed lunch or provide a pre agreed menu, taking account of any dietary requirements. Ensure that you have stocked up on sufficient tea, coffee, milk, juice and snacks, along with enough cups and plates. Tea and coffee could be bought in bulk, to keep costs down and then supplied free, whilst lunch could be charged for separately from the booking fee, as each person will likely have different requirements. Also you could offer a free or reasonably priced nutritious breakfast, available to those who arrive within a specified time before the class begins, which might encourage people to not arrive late and interrupt the class.

Legal Matters

If you are intending to teach classes from within your own home, then the area that you set aside for this purpose should be considered to be a place of business. Contact the appropriate authorities to find out if any restrictions or regulations might apply to the type of course or workshop that you are planning to run. Speak to your insurance provider to determine whether your existing household insurance policy will cover loss or damage to tools, equipment or materials. Arrange insurance to cover against possible claims for injury or damage caused to people or their property when they visit your place of work, such as the students you are teaching. You could also take out insurance to cover loss of income due to ill health. When comparing insurance providers, look for the deals that best suit your requirements and read the small print to ensure you have adequate cover. Seek independent expert advice if you are at all uncertain with regards to any of the legal, insurance, taxation or financial implications of running your own arts and crafts courses or workshops.

Class Planning

When planning the content and structure of classes that you will be running, consider what you expect your students to learn. Provide projects that they can complete on the day, so that they are able to leave with a finished item. You could also supply a worksheet, so that people can track their progress and have a record of the tools, materials and steps required to complete the project. They could then repeat the project again in their own time, perhaps using craft kits that they can purchase from you. Course material could also be made available on your website, for students who have attended the class. The difficulty of what you teach should be suitable for the current experience level of each person. You could offer separate courses for beginner, intermediate or more advanced students, adjusting the content of each class accordingly. This would enable people to progress from beginner to more advanced courses as their level of skill and experience increases.

Depending upon the length of a course or workshop, you could break it up into logical stages, so that students are able to properly absorb what they are learning. Make it clear what time students should arrive, so that they are ready to begin on time. In addition to teaching courses or workshops aimed at people who want to become artists or makers, you could also run events suitable for corporate team building days or social occasions, such as parties. Those attending would be more likely to already know each other and they might have additional objectives, such as developing team working skills or just enjoying a social activity. You should plan classes so that each student enjoys the experience and leaves with a sense of achievement, having learned something new. This could prompt mentions on social media and recommendations to family and friends, helping to attract future bookings.

Teaching Classes

Having properly planned and prepared for the classes that you are going to teach, try to relax and make your students feel welcome when they arrive. Before the class begins, do not spend too much time on introductions and instead create a positive atmosphere in which people feel comfortable getting to know each other as the day progresses. Personalities can sometimes clash and particular individuals might tend to dominate a class, so you should ensure that everyone gets their fair share of attention and no one feels left out. Some students might complete the set project more quickly than others and you could have additional projects available for them to work on. When students struggle to complete a project, it might be appropriate to invite them to attend another class, which will be better suited to their current level of experience. If some students find the projects you provide on a course too easy, then you could recommend more advanced classes.

Take the time to understand the needs of each student, so that you can provide a learning experience which is both relevant and engaging. Rather than overwhelming students with information, observe their progress and move at an appropriate speed. Recalling your own school or college days, you might have found that the classes you enjoyed and learned most from were those in which the teacher made a subject relevant and interesting. Therefore you should try to make what you teach not only informative, but also entertaining, within reason. For example you could share examples from your own creative journey, including times when things went well or others when you struggled to overcome challenges. Every student who completes a piece of work should feel confident they have learned sufficient, that with the necessary tools and materials, they could make the item again on their own.

CHAPTER 15 ORGANISING CRAFT FAIRS

Craft Fairs

There are thousands of artists and makers looking for craft fairs where they can exhibit and sell their work. Many of them struggle however to find suitable events and this has led some to begin running their own craft fairs. You might be an individual who has decided to organise events, where you can sell your own work, in addition to inviting other stallholders. Alternatively you could be a member of an artists and makers group that has decided to organise events at which to exclusively promote and sell work created by their members. The group might have formed online, met in a social situation or when attending craft events. Sharing the workload and costs among a group of people could enable the events to become successful more quickly than when an individual organises events on their own.

Some of what is written in this chapter, for example finding stallholders, might not apply to a cooperative type business, which only sells members work. However, the general advice regarding running successful events would still be relevant. For example it is important to put in place the necessary legal and financial framework and recognise that managing a successful event requires the investment of sufficient resources. Having enough time to create and sell their own work might require an individual to find someone else to help with the event management, whilst among a group each member could take their turn at running the events. Over time a supportive community of sellers could be established, attracting a growing number of buyers, who are looking for premium handmade items, either as gifts or for their own use.

Event Finances

When you run your first craft fair, the upfront costs will require an initial investment and you might not begin generating a profit until you have run a number of events. It is therefore essential to manage cash flow effectively and you could seek financial advice from your accountant. Depending upon the size of the venue booked, you could look for perhaps a dozen stallholders at your first few events or twenty to thirty if there is sufficient available space. The main costs are likely to include hiring the venue, insurance, marketing materials and advertising. You might also have to pay staff wages if you decide to hire other people to work at the event. The main source of income will come from money that exhibitors pay to book their craft stalls. Charging visitors an entrance fee might bring in some additional revenue, but it could also reduce visitor numbers. However, if you ask for a small entrance fee you could include a free tea or coffee. Your aim should be to establish a reputation for running successful events, which attract a good number of visitors and where stallholders are able to make enough sales to have a profitable day. This could enable you to attract increasing numbers of stallholders wanting to book tables at your future events.

As an organiser running a small event with perhaps a few dozen stallholders you might charge them each around thirty to fifty pounds per table. An organiser running a well promoted event, held at a prestigious venue, that attracts hundreds of stallholders and thousands of visitors, could charge exhibitors hundreds of pounds per table per day. Although a visitor entry fee would require personnel to manage the process and could reduce footfall, a well established event could still attract many visitors. In addition to the potential for additional income, a benefit of charging an entry fee is being able to offer free or discounted entry as an incentive to some visitors. Event organisers might also be able to justify charging visitors an entry fee, by providing additional entertainment or attractions on the day and because of the high standard of the venue facilities.

Insurance

When running a craft fair, organisers must be aware of their legal obligations and ensure that they have taken out the necessary insurance, with adequate cover for any claims made against them by a third party. This would include insurance against accidents, property damage or personal injury. When you are running an event, you should expect that those managing the venue will ask you to provide evidence that you have obtained the necessary insurance. Contact your insurers regarding the insurance status of any personal vehicles that you use for work, as your existing policy might not cover this. You could enquire about insurance to provide you with cover if an event has to be cancelled, perhaps due to adverse weather conditions, along with cover for equipment that is lost or damaged. If you intend running a large number of events, then having a policy providing cover for multiple events could reduce the overall cost. If you are going to be assisted by volunteers or paid staff, then you should also look into any insurance requirements.

Confirm that the venue you intend hiring is properly insured, although this will be to cover them rather than you. Inform stallholders who are booking tables at events you run that they will need to obtain the necessary insurance to cover them against claims made for damage or injury due to their stall or their products. Anyone preparing and selling food should have obtained the appropriate documentation and abide by food hygiene regulations. Provide exhibitors with relevant details, such as your name, business address, email address and telephone number, so that they can contact you with questions about the event and any licensing requirements that they must comply with. You could look for a broker experienced in providing insurance for arts and crafts related events and have a written risk assessment carried out, without which an insurer might not pay if a claim is made. To ensure that you comply with all legal requirements, you could seek expert advice.

Finding a Venue

Finding an appropriate venue at which to run your events is essential. You might decide to hire a small venue for your first few events, until you gain some experience and feel confident enough to move on to somewhere larger. Factors to consider when choosing a venue include the potential number of stallholders and expected visitor numbers. Also look at transport links, passing trade, onsite facilities and the availability of parking for stallholders and visitors. A limited number of suitable local venues and the size of your budget could also place constraints upon your options.

You might already know of somewhere suitable to host events, in which case you could enquire with the venue manager about available dates. Alternatively you could search online, draw up a shortlist and then arrange to visit each venue and view the facilities. The owners of a venue might welcome the opportunity to hire their property to an event organiser, for an appropriate fee, particularly if there was the potential for it to become a regular source of additional revenue for them. They might also want to increase their profits by providing services such as onsite catering. Ensure that relevant contracts are agreed and signed before you begin promoting events.

If you have previously attended crafts fairs as an exhibitor, you might have gained some insight into what is involved in running them. However, when you are organising an event you will be taking on the responsibility of making it a success, not just for yourself, but also for each stall holder and visitor. Ask yourself which events that you have attended in the past you thought were well run and why. Carry out some market research, asking people about their past experience either as an exhibitor or when visiting a craft fair. You could also attend events held at venues you are considering hiring and speak to people you meet, listening carefully to any feedback they give you.

When you run craft fairs during the autumn or winter months, you will probably want to hold them indoors. Although during the spring and summer you could hold events outside, on parkland for example, the unpredictability of the weather might make it advisable to hire a marquee.

You might find a country show or festival, attracting hundreds or even thousands of visitors at which you could run your craft fairs. However, you should carefully calculate the costs involved and the potential profit.

Date and Time

Small craft fairs are typically held for one day, though larger events could be run on two or more days. Holding events at regular intervals, such as the same time every Tuesday or on the first Saturday of each month, could make them a fixture in the calendars of stallholders and visitors. When running a number of events at the same venue, you could reduce costs by reusing banners, posters and leaflets, if for example you have printed on them 'this coming Saturday' rather than a specific date. Craft fairs typically open to the public around mid morning and close late afternoon, which allows time for the stall holders to set up before visitors arrive and pack away by a reasonable time after they have left. You could request that stallholders do not begin packing up earlier than a specified time.

When you are deciding on the date and time to run your events, consider any other nearby visitor attractions open on the same date, which could either increase passing trade or, if they compete for visitors, reduce footfall. Although there are craft fairs held throughout the year, the number grows during the spring and summer months, when they are often held outdoors, to take advantage of the warmer weather and additional hours of daylight. Craft fairs are also popular in November and December, during the weeks before Christmas, with events often held in the evening, when visitors can browse for festive items and gifts, enjoying the seasonal atmosphere.

Finding Stallholders

When you are inviting exhibitors to book craft stalls, provide them with a convenient, easy to follow process. Online or printed booking forms should include relevant terms and conditions. Also make it easy for people to pay using their preferred payment method. Maintaining a good standard of exhibitor work at your events, would need a quality control process, which could involve you reviewing work made by exhibitors, before agreeing to them booking a stall. This might require exhibitors to send by email photographs of their work and their table display, or post samples of what they make. You would then be able to judge the quality of their work, to ensure that it reaches an appropriate standard.

During the planning of your events think carefully about what will appeal to visitors and give stallholders the best chance of finding customers for their work. For example having exhibitors who are each selling a different type of art or craft would give visitors a greater choice of items to buy. Exhibitors could be selling exclusively handmade items or you might also allow some quality vintage stalls. Events that you organise could be promoted online and within suitable print publications, raising awareness among exhibitors, as well as visitors looking for events to attend.

Event Marketing

The choice of a good venue at a suitable location should help to attract visitors to an event, however effective marketing will also be needed to raise awareness with the target audience and increase footfall. Even with a limited budget you can still make use of online advertising, social media and word of mouth to raise the profile of your events. Exhibitors who have paid to have a stall at a craft fair will be disappointed if low visitor numbers result in them having few sales and this could make them less likely to book stalls at your future events. If you are running events with a group of other artists and makers, attracting sufficient potential customers on the day could contribute to your long term success.

Having an event name which is descriptive and memorable will be an asset, as are positive mission and vision statements that reflect your business brand. Maintaining a consistent image across all marketing materials and communications will help to strengthen your brand identity in the minds of the public. Approach local media with interesting stories that would appeal to their respective audiences. Leaflets could be distributed in the local area and permission sought to put notices in local shops, community centres or libraries. Remember to provide contact details within your marketing material. You could also include QR codes, taking people to landing pages on your website.

The more that you charge stallholders, the higher will be their expectations and the greater the need to attract visitors who will want to buy their work. Also remember that in addition to sales on the day of the event, artists and makers will want to market their work, which could lead to future sales or commissions. If the work that stallholders will be selling is similar in some way, the event might lend itself to having a theme. For example the event could be promoted as reflecting a particular period of history or contemporary lifestyle, such as sustainable living and recycling. Ensure that you include relevant information in marketing materials, such as when and where the event is taking place.

You could arrange entertainment, such as performance artists, musicians playing live music, or creative workshops. There could be stalls selling regional or specialist food and attractions, such as fairground games. Although the planning and organisation required would involve additional effort and cost, it could help to create more of a festival atmosphere and attract a larger number of visitors. The event could be photographed and video recorded, for use in print, online and broadcast media marketing campaigns. After the event, video footage could be edited to create material for sharing on social media and embedded within your website. You could include interviews with stallholders and visitors, after requesting their permission by asking them to sign release forms. Photographs taken during the day could be used in newsletters or blog posts about the event and marketing material promoting future events.

Directional Signs

When people are unfamiliar with the area where a venue is located, they might struggle to find it. Therefore, on the day of the event, placing directional signs in relevant positions at the approaches to the venue, could help stallholders and visitors find the event venue. The purpose of such signs is to improve traffic flow and not to advertise the event and signs must not pose a hazard. During the months before an event is due to take place, you should contact the appropriate authorities, to ensure that you are aware of what must be done to comply with the relevant legal requirements. Find out how to go about applying for permission to use temporary directional signs and any restrictions that you need to be aware of. For example the appearance and wording that you are allowed to use, how long before an event begins you can put signs up and when they must be removed.

Before The Event

Ensure that you confirm bookings, manage payments and handle all relevant paperwork. Draw a floor plan of the venue, which shows the position of each stall and relevant information such as the exhibitor names and what they each make. During the weeks leading up to an event, send a reminder email to each exhibitor that has booked a stall, confirming the date, time and venue location. Attach a map with clear directions to the venue and a copy of the floor plan of the craft fair. Also provide important information such as parking arrangements and what time exhibitors can arrive to begin setting up their stalls, including any requirements they need to be aware of. If you are able to gain access to the venue the day before the event, then you could begin the setup process, reducing your workload on the day of the event. For example you could put up tables, position name cards for each stall, attach floor plans at the entrances and ensure the venue is ready to receive stallholders and visitors when they begin arriving.

Event Day

On the day of the event, you should arrive early to carry out any necessary preparations before the stallholders begin arriving. Either you or someone working with you, should be on hand to greet exhibitors as they arrive and available to answer any questions that they might have during the day. However, if you are running an event along with a group of other artists and makers, then each member of the group could agree to take their turn at managing the events. This would enable the other members to focus on setting up their stalls and selling their work. When someone is running an event and not available to look after their own stall, they could be financially compensated or ask family and friends to run their stall for them.

Exhibitors who have booked a stall, will expect you to have found a suitable venue. You should be able to demonstrate that you have done what is reasonable to promote the event and attract visitors on the day. However, the events that you run could still be affected by factors beyond your control, such as the weather. Also some stallholders will probably have greater success on the day than others, which will in part depend upon how well they prepare for the day, what they are selling, their pricing and how well they engage with potential customers. Make an effort to speak both to stallholders and visitors during the day, to find out how the day went for them and whether they might want to attend future events. This provides an opportunity for you to carry out some informal market research and address any issues or misunderstandings.

After The Event

After you have run a craft fair, you should determine if it was a success. For example did the event produce a profit, loss or break even. Evaluate the effectiveness of the event marketing and decide whether you would want to run more events at the same venue or try a different venue. Review feedback and market research findings, so that you are aware of any potential improvements that could be made when running future events. Send a thank you email to anyone who assisted you with the promotion or management of the event. Also thank stallholders and any visitors that you spoke to, if they agreed to receiving communications from you. Tell people that you look forward to seeing them at your next craft fair and send reminders when you have confirmed the date, time and venue for events that you will be running in the future.

CLOSING THOUGHTS

Running your own business can be a rewarding experience. Rather than waiting for other people to tell you what to do or trusting in luck, you have the opportunity to take control of your life and follow a path of your own choosing. Having devoted the time necessary to develop skills in your chosen art or craft, a positive outlook combined with hard work, will help you on your path to creative freedom and financial independence. Few people become famous and accumulate great wealth, but earning a good living doing something that you love will help you to find personal fulfilment and success on your own terms. This can provide your life with a deeper sense of meaning, purpose and direction in a rapidly changing world, bringing greater happiness both to yourself and those around you.

ACKNOWLEDGEMENTS

The family business that we built together provided me with the inspiration to write this book. Thank you all for your support, encouragement and help.

ABOUT THE AUTHOR

Paul Riley is one of the founders of UKCraftFairs, a family run business promoting arts and crafts. His other interests include history, art and design, the creative process and sustainable technology.

Printed in Great Britain
by Amazon